Milan

T0384095

As a main urban centre of one of the most dynamic European regions, Milan is a key location from which to study narratives of innovations and contemporary productions – old and new manufacturing, tertiary and consumptive sectors, creative and cultural economy – and investigate their influence both on spatial patterns and urban policy agenda.

Accordingly, this book explores the contentious geographies of innovation, productions and working spaces, both empirically and theoretically in a city that, since the beginning of the 2000s, has been involved in a process of urban change, with relevant spatial and socio-economic effects, within an increasingly turbulent world economy. Through this analysis, the book provides an insight into the complexity of contemporary urban phenomena beyond a traditional metropolitan lens, highlighting issues such as rescaling, urban decentralization and recentralization, extensive urban transformation and shrinkage and molecular urban regeneration.

This book is a valuable resource for academics, researchers and scholars focusing on Urban Studies such as Urban Policy, Urban Planning, Urban Geography, Urban Economy and Urban Sociology.

Simonetta Armondi is a researcher in political and economic geography, and Professor of Urban and Regional Analysis at the Politecnico di Milano, Italy. Her research and teaching activities focus on the geography of urban change related to economic restructuring, contemporary capitalisms and urban policies.

Stefano Di Vita is Research Fellow and adjunct Professor at the Politecnico di Milano, Italy, where he carries out research and teaching activities in the fields of regional and urban planning and design. His main interests concern phenomena and tools of urban change processes supported by both ordinary and extraordinary projects.

Built Environment City Studies

The *Built Environment City Studies* series provides researchers and academics with a detailed look at individual cities through a specific lens. These concise books delve into a case study of an international city, focusing on a key built environment topic. Written by scholars from around the world, the collection provides a library of thorough studies into trends, developments and approaches that affect our cities.

Seville: Through the Urban Void
Miguel Torres

Amman: Gulf Capital, Identity, and Contemporary Megaprojects
Majd Musa

Baltimore: Reinventing an Industrial Legacy City
Klaus Philipsen

Milan: Productions, Spatial Patterns and Urban Change
Edited by Simonetta Armondi and Stefano Di Vita

Milan

Productions, Spatial Patterns
and Urban Change

**Edited by
Simonetta Armondi
and Stefano Di Vita**

Routledge
Taylor & Francis Group

LONDON AND NEW YORK

First published 2018
by Routledge
4 Park Square, Milton Park, Abingdon, Oxon OX14 4RN

and by Routledge
605 Third Avenue, New York, NY 10017

First issued in paperback 2022

Routledge is an imprint of the Taylor & Francis Group, an informa business

This book is the result of a collaboration between the research hub "Innovation, Productions and Urban Space" of the Department of Architecture and Urban Studies at the Politecnico di Milano and the Centro Studi PIM.

Trademark notice: Product or corporate names may be trademarks or registered trademarks, and are used only for identification and explanation without intent to infringe.

Publisher's Note
The publisher has gone to great lengths to ensure the quality of this reprint but points out that some imperfections in the original copies may be apparent.

British Library Cataloguing-in-Publication Data
A catalogue record for this book is available from the British Library

Library of Congress Cataloging-in-Publication Data
Names: Armondi, Simonetta, editor.
Title: Milan : productions, spatial patterns and urban change / edited by Simonetta Armondi and Stefano Di Vita.
Other titles: Milan (Routledge Firm)
Description: New York : Routledge, 2017. | Series: Built environment city studies | Includes bibliographical references and index.
Identifiers: LCCN 2017025146 | ISBN 9781138244795 (hb) | ISBN 9781315269450 (ebook)
Subjects: LCSH: City planning—Italy—Milan. | Urbanization—Italy—Milan.
Classification: LCC HT169.I82 M555 2017 | DDC 307.1/2160945211—dc23
LC record available at https://lccn.loc.gov/2017025146

ISBN 13: 978-1-03-247669-8 (pbk)
ISBN 13: 978-1-138-24479-5 (hbk)
ISBN 13: 978-1-315-26945-0 (ebk)

DOI: 10.4324/9781315269450

Typeset in Times New Roman
by Apex CoVantage, LLC

Contents

Figures

Tables

Contributors

Simonetta Armondi (PhD in Environmental and Territorial Planning, Politecnico di Milano) is Assistant Professor in Economic-Political Geography. She teaches Urban and Regional Analysis at the Politecnico di Milano. Her research and teaching activities focus on one side on urban change and economic restructuring related to contemporary rescaling, on the other side on public policies, in which old and new spatial narratives are mobilized.

Matteo Bolocan Goldstein (PhD in Public territorial policies, IUAV, Venezia) is a full professor of Economic-Political Geography and is currently President of Centro Studi PIM – Programmazione Intercomunale dell'area Metropolitana. For the last several years, his research has involved theoretical and empirical work focused on the interpretation of urbanization processes and the urban space metamorphosis with particular regard to the Milanese context.

Antonella Bruzzese (PhD in Environmental and Territorial Planning, Politecnico di Milano) is Associate Professor in Urban Design at the Politecnico di Milano. Her research interests focus on public space, on strategies and processes of place making and on the role of creative industries in urban regeneration with attention to the synergies between the project of physical transformation and urban policies.

Stefano Di Vita (PhD in Urban, Regional and Environmental Planning, Politecnico di Milano) is a research fellow and contract professor at the Politecnico di Milano, where he carries out teaching and research activities in the fields of regional and urban planning and design. His main research interests concern issues related to sustainability and smartness of urban change processes.

Ilaria Mariotti (PhD in Economic Geography, University of Groningen) is Associate Professor in Regional Economics at the Politecnico di Milano.

Her main research interests concern location theory, agglomeration economics and industrial districts, the internationalization of manufacturing and transport and logistics industries and the effects of internationalization on the home and host countries.

Corinna Morandi (Architect, Politecnico di Milano) is Full Professor in Town Planning and Urban Design at the Politecnico di Milano. Her main research areas concern town planning in the metropolitan area of Milan and the role of commercial and multifunctional poles in urban dynamics. She is a member of the International PhD course in Urban Planning, Design and Policy, at the Politecnico di Milano.

Carolina Pacchi (PhD in Urban and Environmental Planning, Politecnico di Milano) is Associate Professor at the Politecnico di Milano, where she teaches Planning Theory and Practice and Local Conflict Resolution, and she is involved in research activities on urban governance, planning strategies based on stakeholder involvement and different forms of grassroots social innovation at the local level.

Mario Paris (PhD in Urban and Regional Planning, Universidad de Valladolid) Since 2006, he has worked with Laboratorio Urb&Com as a researcher and consultant; he collaborates with IUU de la Universidad de Valladolid. He is also Contract Professor of Urban Planning in Politecnico di Milano. In 2015, he was validated as Urbact ad-hoc expert and since 2016 has been International Fellow in the Department of Architecture and Urban Studies, Politecnico di Milano.

Gabriele Pasqui (PhD in Public territorial policies, IUAV, Venezia) is Director of the Department of Architecture and Urban Studies, Politecnico di Milano. Full Professor of Urban Policies, his key scientific interests include interpretations of contemporary cities dynamics, urban conflicts, urban populations, local development policies, strategic planning, urban governance and policies.

Andrea Rolando (PhD in Representation of the Built Environment, Università di Roma La Sapienza) is a full professor at the Politecnico in Milano, Department of Architecture and Urban Studies, where he researches and teaches in the fields of analysis and representation of urban and regional phenomena, with specific focus on the changes occurring in the region between Torino and Milano and on the relationship between spatial quality and infrastructures.

Introduction

Simonetta Armondi and Stefano Di Vita

This edited book aims at providing an unprecedented observation of contemporary urban processes in Milan using English text for worldwide accessibility, and through its multidisciplinary approach, in relation to its different authors; its trans-scalar approach, in relation to specific contents of different chapters. Indeed, this analysis articulates within several spatial focuses, defined according to specific issues, by ignoring administrative borders, which are no more adequate to current urban phenomena, differently extended from the dense urban core to the wider urban region.

On the occasion of this statement about the Milan case study, this manuscript aims at pinpointing a significant contribution to the current international debate concerning, in particular, two issues:

• the innovation in global urban change processes according to a long-standing world crisis and a related re-organization of spatial and socio-economic dynamics;
• the innovation in global urban space definitions on the background of a growing planetary urbanization and a related upsize of cities.

First, the book assigns to the urban change a critical meaning in relation to new productions, their related workplaces and social practices, with reference to the broad theoretical framework on knowledge, creative and sharing economy, urban technologies, smart urbanism, and post-networked city (Florida, 2005; Cook and Lazzaretti, 2008; Komninos, 2008; Madanipour, 2011; Gill Garcia Pardo and Nam, 2015; Carrillo et al., 2015; Coutard and Rutherford, 2015). Second, the book takes an urban space definition that refers to new socio-economic dynamics, against the backdrop of the recent academic debate on the world urbanization (Brenner and Schmid, 2015), or on the multifaceted category of agglomeration and the limits of the urban theory (Scott and Storper, 2015; Cavallo et al., 2014).

This last debate has been going on for years according to the growing regional and macro-regional scale of contemporary cities (Scott, 2001; Hall and Pain, 2006; Soja, 2011; Brenner, 2014), and to renewed demands for a new development model, also expressed by the current world crisis (Rydin, 2013). However, at present this scientific and cultural discussion cannot ignore the ongoing worldwide rise of new nationalisms, corresponding to a growing reaction to globalization, the spatial and socio-economic effects of which will manifest in the following years. This is the result of divisions produced by an increasingly city-centric competitiveness agenda, driven by globalization and free trade, between growing concentration of economic opportunities on (regionalized) urban nodes and the "rest" outside or in-between these nodes, recently politically energized by populist narratives (Herrschel and Newman, 2017). This phenomenon, that since 2016 has been mainly expressed through Brexit in the UK and Trump's election in the US, is aimed at re-strengthening national borders, undermining those world urban networks (Taylor, 2004, 2013) that have been developing without limits at a global level since at least the fall of the Berlin Wall in 1989. Therefore, according to this world scenario (where the future of the European Union is obfuscated also), the outcomes of projects and processes described by this manuscript concerning the case of Milan, already defined as a node of global networks, are increasingly uncertain.

On this strongly unstable background, as it is impossible to find and identify shared scholarly concepts and clear definitions of different forms of urban innovations, this book provides a representation of some of their – current and potential – spatial manifestations related to "production" issues. According to the ongoing development of ICTs, and their effects on spatial and socio-economic dynamics, the term production now needs to refer to economic activities, in which the separation between manufacturing, service and retail sectors is blurred. Therefore, this manuscript highlights contributions, which critically engage in dealing with the nexus between productions (of goods and/or services) and urban change. In particular, by dealing with different indicators and "symptoms" of urban innovations, it specifically aims at reflecting about current urban spatiality and geographies of contemporary productive activities and related workplaces, in order to advance the academic debate and learnings concerning urban processes connected to (apparently self-evident or unintended) socio-economic advances.

Regarding the contents of its ten chapters, the book needs to develop theoretical frameworks, through which the nature of the nexus between productions and urban change can be theorized. Therefore, the manuscript first of all emphasizes which Milan urban change phenomena it delineates (Chapter 1, by Simonetta Armondi and Stefano Di Vita). At the same time, it explores the ways in which "narratives" about contemporary productive activities and workplaces are being rolled out across contradictory spatial and socio-economic processes within the Milan urban region (Chapter 2 by Matteo Bolocan Goldstein). The book deals with both the major and minor ways in which such productive activities constitute material spaces and shape, respectively, trans-scalar socio-economic networks (Chapter 3 by Ilaria Mariotti), creative production practices related to urban regeneration (Chapter 4 by Antonella Bruzzese), and hybrid workplaces of the contemporary sharing economy (Chapter 5 by Carolina Pacchi). These issues are focused also by discussing how projects for productive spaces relate to urban patterns and place-making.

After these introductive and thematic chapters, the manuscript articulates the observation and interpretation of the nexus between new productions and urban change according to some specific places of the Milan urban region, which are identified independently from their administrative articulation, but looking at the spatial development of the investigated phenomena. A first comparison between nodes of trans-scalar knowledge-based networks focuses on the southern area of the Milan urban core, which is a city sector only recently involved within a wide urban change process based on the development of new centralities (Chapter 6 by Corinna Morandi and Mario Paris). Besides, the book investigates the ways in which old and new production narratives establish roots in Milan's specific contexts, also renovating the trans-scalar relationships between the dense urban core and the wider urban region. On the one hand, it deals with the North East and the North West Milan (respectively, Chapter 7 by Simonetta Armondi and Chapter 8 by Stefano Di Vita). On the other, it focuses on the potential ways in which different forms of urban innovation, led by current spatial and socio-economic dynamics, intersect the recent and multi-layer infrastructural development, that has been providing new relations with and within the Milan urban region: from suburban to high-speed train systems (Chapter 9 by Andrea Rolando).

Finally, the book closes with an in-depth analysis of the Milan urban agenda, focusing on both necessary trans-scalar strategies and urban policies, also implying changing geometries of power. This is, from the small Milan Municipality, to the broader new Milan Metropolitan City, up to the even wider urban region, although this is still divided within different authorities from the administrative point of view (Chapter 10 by Gabriele Pasqui).

This manuscript investigates and represents these multifaceted issues through a deep observation of places within the compact core of the Milan urban region – that is, the Milan municipality and its closest surroundings – by bringing together multidisciplinary and trans-scalar contributions, which explore the ongoing dynamics of productions and workspaces both theoretically and empirically. Therefore, the empirical milieu is the current and wide Milan urban change process, which is ongoing despite the local effects of the global crisis in the last decade, even by crisscrossing the municipal borders of the main city. Indeed, the Milan urban region corresponds to the Italian economic capital, as well as one of the crucial European nodes of world urban networks (OECD, 2006), that has been recently strengthened by – but not only – the Expo 2015 (Bolocan Goldstein, 2015; Pasqui, 2016; Bruzzese and Di Vita, 2016). Thus, even with its local specificities, Milan represents an interesting case study, both according to its urban dynamics and their regional-scale spatiality, as well as to its role of European gate city towards developing countries in Africa and Asia, according to both its geographical location and the (still uncertain) post-Brexit scenario.

Within this frame, the manuscript offers an original multidisciplinary and trans-scalar observation and interpretation of contemporary urban phenomena by verifying urban effects of innovations in production activities within one of the most (at present) meaningful and representative European cases such as the one of Milan. In this regard, it offers an original, up-to-date advancement in comparison to other studies and publications concerning the ongoing Milan urban change, which were promoted before the breaking out of the global crisis in 2008 and the development of its urban effects in the following years. Moreover, this is the first international book entirely focused on the current urban dynamics of Milan, which is and has been the most important Italian urban region for decades in terms of population, wealth, employment, and manufacturing activities. The book therefore describes the reasons for which this urban region has been maintaining a leading position in Italy in terms of investments, entrepreneurships, technological progress, social innovation, and urban transformations since the Italian unification in 1861 and, in particular, the end of the Second World War.

According to these contents and spatial contexts, the books is oriented by the following main objectives:

- To question the role that new productive activities and workplaces play in moulding new forms of urban change in the implosion/explosion of the city (Brenner, 2014), and how these eventually relate to the current political agenda. That is, also by underlining evidences, contradictions, and tensions in how these new productions and working spaces are being mobilized by different public and private actors.
- To provide the first chance, accessible worldwide, for representing the complexity of the contemporary urban phenomena within the specific Milan spatial context. That is, one of the main and most meaningful spatial and productive platforms in Europe. On the one hand, as it is crossed by opposed tensions and impulses (such as urban decentralization and

recentralization; intensive and extensive urban transformations; urban change through both shrinkage and regeneration processes; city of consumptions and productions). On the other hand, as it is not only related to fashion and design, but also to other economic activities, even characterized by medium-high and high technological intensity (such as pharmaceutical, chemical, mechanics, electric, electronic and optics, rubber and plastic productions, and publishing).

- To promote a multidisciplinary observation and interpretation of the contemporary urban phenomena by integrating urban policy, planning and design approaches, with ones of urban economy, geography, and spatial representation.
- To observe and critically interpret ongoing transformations through a trans-scalar spatial lens and, consequently, to explore the development of new spatial geographies and patterns concerning productions and working spaces, and related uses. Thus, by dealing with effects of both large-scale and molecular practices and projects of urban change, connected to new economic activities (often based on digital technologies) and related social practices.
- To challenge traditional interpretative categories and assumptions concerning the urban dynamics and dimensions, starting from both the effects of the global crisis and the path dependency of the Milan urban region development.

References

Bolocan Goldstein, M. (2015). Post-expo geographical scenarios. *Urbanistica*, 155, pp. 118–122.

Brenner, N. ed. (2014). *Implosions/explosions: Towards a study of planetary urbanization*. Berlin: Jovis Verlag.

Brenner, N. and Schmid, C. (2015). Towards a new epistemology of the urban. *City*, 19(2–3), pp. 151–182.

Bruzzese, A. and Di Vita, S. eds. (2016). Expo 2015 and its legacies. *Territorio*, 77, pp. 67–109.

Carrillo, F.J., Yigitcanlar, T., Garcia, B. and Lonnqvist, A. (2015). *Knowledge and the city: Concepts, applications and trends of knowledge-based urban development*. London, New York: Routledge.

Cavallo, R., Komossa, S., Marzot, N., Berghauser Pont, M. and Kuijper, J. (2014). *New urban configurations*. Amsterdam: IOS Press.

Cook, P. and Lazzaretti, L. (2008). *Creative cities, cultural clusters and local economic development*. Cheltenham: Edward Elgar.

Coutard, O. and Rutheford, J. (2015). *Beyond the networked city: Infrastructure reconfigurations and urban change in the North and South*. London, New York: Routledge.

Florida, R. (2005). *Cities and the creative class*. London, New York: Routledge.

Gill Garcia, J.R., Pardo, T.A. and Nam, T. (2015). *Smarter as the new urban agenda: A comprehensive view of the 21st century city*. New York: Springer.

Hall, P. and Pain, K. eds. (2006). *The polycentric metropolis: Learning from mega-city regions in Europe*. London: Earthscan.

Herrschel, T. and Newman, P. (2017). *Cities as international actors: Urban and regional governance beyond the nation state*. London: Palgrave MacMillan.

Komninos, N. (2008). *Intelligent cities and globalization of innovation networks*. London, New York: Routledge.

Madanipour, A. (2011). *Knowledge economy and the city*. London, New York: Routledge.

OECD. (2006). *OECD territorial reviews: Milan, Italy*. Paris: OECD Publishing.

Pasqui, G. (2016). Expo 2015 and Milan: Interwined stories. *Urbanistica*, 155, pp. 106–109.

Rydin, Y. (2013). *The future of planning: Beyond growth dependence*. Bristol: University of Bristol Policy Press.

Scott, A.J. ed. (2001). *Global city-regions: Trends, theory, policy*. Oxford: Oxford University Press.

Scott, A.J. and Storper, M. (2015). The nature of cities: The scope and limits of urban theory. *International Journal of Urban and Regional Research*, 39(1), pp. 1–15.

Soja, E.D. (2011). Regional urbanization and the end of metropolitan era. In: G. Bridge and S. Watson, eds., *The new Blackwell companion to the city*. Hoboken: Wiley-Blackwell, pp. 679–689.

Taylor, P.J. (2004). *World city network. A global urban analysis*. London, New York: Routledge.

Taylor, P.J. (2013). *Extraordinary cities: Millennia of moral syndromes, world-system and city/state relations*. Cheltenham: Edward Elgar.

1 Which Milan?

Setting the scene for reflecting urban decline, resilience, and change

Simonetta Armondi and Stefano Di Vita

Introduction

As already mentioned in the Introduction, there are several reasons the spatial focus of this manuscript – first aimed at understanding the role played by new productive activities and workplaces in the urban change processes and, therefore, in urban planning and policy activities – is the Milan urban region (paying specific attention to its densest urban core). For instance, on the one hand, the innovative spatial and socio-economic dynamics promoted in one of the main and most meaningful spatial and productive platform in Europe within a longstanding world economic crisis. On the other, the opposite tensions and impulses – such as decentralization and recentralization projects; intensive and extensive urban transformations; urban shrinkage and regeneration processes; city of consumption and production's development models – which are changing the traditional perception of the urban space. From the centrifugal socio-spatial dynamics of the dense urban core, to the centripetal socio-spatial dynamics of the wider urban region,[1] also within the perspective of a future strengthening of the new Milan Metropolitan City authority.[2] Therefore, this first chapter aims at "setting the scene" in order to define and represent the spatial, socio-economic, and political context, which all the other chapters refer to, as well as through the contribution of maps elaborated by the *Centro Studi PIM*, which are included in a dedicated section following this first contribution by the manuscript editors.

Spatial pattern, economic geography, and urban governance

Milan is an interesting case study because of the specificities of its spatial and socio-economic dynamics and its public policies, which make this city and its urban region able to represent the complexity of current world urban phenomena. In fact, Milan – "land in the middle", following its etymological root *Mediolanum* – is currently the functional-economic capital of a wider city-region that extends to the entire Northern Italy macro-region,[3] with more than 23 million inhabitants (Figure 1.2). If we consider Northern Italy as a global city-region (Perulli and Pichierri, 2010), it would be counted up among the first places (Scott, 2001). Milan (and its administrative region, Lombardy) is also part of a wider supranational network of European economic engines, including Stuttgart (and the federated State of Baden-Wurttemberg, in Germany), Lyon (and the administrative region of Rhone-Alpes, in France), and Barcelona (and the autonomous community of Catalonia, in Spain) (Figure 1.1). The macro-regional, national, and European connections of the city are even stronger, with infrastructural corridors (motorways, railways, and high-speed railways) linking Milan to:

• at the macro-regional and national level, Bologna-Florence-Rome-Naples, Genoa, Turin, and Venice-Padua-Treviso, (Figure 1.2);
• at the international level, the main European urban nodes, being the city located along the European corridor 5 (Seville-Kiev), and close to the European corridors 1 (Berlin-Palermo, crossing the corridor 5 in Verona, west of Milan) and 24 (Genoa-Rotterdam, crossing the corridor 5 in Novara, east of Milan) (Figure 1.1), all under development.

After the Fordist de-industrialization phase, which took place in the 1970s and 1980s, with the proliferation of vacant industrial areas (Figure 1.6), the city has displayed a significant degree of adaptability, with a persisting diversity of economic sectors and with a noteworthy quota of manufacturing industry (Figure 1.4), in particular in the urban region, outside the urban core (OECD, 2006; Balducci, Fedeli and Pasqui, 2011). These two phenomena combined have contributed to boost the resilience of the urban region and to limit job loss process. In the years between the 1990s and the explosion of the economic crisis in 2008, the city has maintained a trend of growth, especially in comparison with other former industrial cities in Italy and in Western countries. Nevertheless, this growth had been more sustained before 2000 (around 3 per cent), but weaker afterwards, between 2000 and the first sign of economic turbulence in 2007[4] (Cucca and Ranci, 2017).

Within this dynamic and resilient context, Milan shows a contradiction between a vital economic base, on the one hand, and a low policy and vision, on the other. In fact, also according to the complexity of public and private actors, the governance of Milan is grounded on a series of loosely coupled institutionalized experiments in the metropolitan area (Gualini, 2003). That is, for instance, from the Milan Intermunicipal Plan designed by Giancarlo

De Carlo in 1963–1965, to the Strategic Project "Città di Città", approved by the former Milan Province in 2006 (Balducci, Fedeli and Pasqui, 2011). As a consequence, Milan has confirmed its reputation as a "polyarchic city" (Dente, Bobbio and Spada, 2005), not linked to just a unique centre of power, in which the governance coalition, the interplay of actors, and the interests in the urban making and remaking have always been complex, multi-layered, and multi-faceted (Perulli, 2016).

Milan is a case of centre without centralization (Perulli, 2014); a radial model whose expansions had origins following the railways infrastructures, mainly towards the North of the city.[5] Accordingly, industries grew in Sesto San Giovanni and in the Brianza area, close to the main city, as well as in nearby cities located further away, such as Bergamo and Brescia. This process was gradual. For instance, firms such as Breda and Pirelli opened their first factories in the surroundings of the Milan railway stations, but at the beginning of the twentieth century, they moved to Sesto San Giovanni in order to exploit larger spaces and workforce.[6]

After, in particular, the Second World War, the city and its urban region affirmed themselves as the main driving area of the economic and demographic boom of the whole country,[7] mainly based on a diversified system of manufacturing activities. Whilst the industrial and residential growth of the Milan municipal area and the northern (highly urbanized) sector of its urban region was impressive (Figure 1.4 and Figure 1.5), no wider scale planning tools or visions were officially approved to orient and manage this mainly spontaneous process. The effects of the lack of planning tools and visions at the urban region scale are visible in the chaotic, disordered, and poor development of the city and its surroundings. This phase of economic and demographic growth of both the Milan municipality and its metropolitan area concluded in the 1970s, when a new phenomenon of production and residential relocation from the main city to the neighbouring municipalities and the external areas of the urban region started (together with a global relocation of economic activities).

As in other European metropolises, at the beginning of the 1980s a new phase started, leading to a service sector metamorphosis and a real estate development of the city (before the 2008 global crisis), and to the current reorganization and innovation of its urban change process (during and beyond the recent economic downturn). This process – that spread from the urban core to the surrounding areas – contributed to substituting both former large industrial plants and small manufacturing buildings with new urban functions and activities (Figure 1.6 and Figure 1.7). Nevertheless, until now, it has been developed without the support of a broad and shared vision (Morandi, 2007), and it still demands for a planning system and a strategic approach able to face to the regional size of spatial and socio-economic dynamics of the city. Consequently, even though the limits and weaknesses of this process the Milan city centre (directly connected to other global cities) has been consolidating as a sort of Italian main epicentre for the current metamorphosis towards a knowledge and creative economy and society. On the contrary, this change has not yet involved the entire urban region, which is still formed by areas affected by "poor metropolitanization" (Centro Studi PIM, 2016). Accordingly, there are several potentialities for the new Milan Metropolitan City to deal with a contentious metropolitanization phenomenon, at the same time made by excellences and poorness, even though effective contributions by this new local authority have been weak until now.[8]

While the Metropolitan Strategic Plan – approved by the new Milan Metropolitan City in 2016 – represents a first proposal for the development of a broad and shared scenario from an innovative perspective, outside of the Milan municipality, this tool had already been anticipated by still "milano-centric" visions. From the "Documento Direttore del Progetto Passante" to the "Documento di Inquadramento Ricostruire la Grande Milano", approved by the Milan City Council in 1984 and in 2000 respectively. According to these plans, the priority axis for the development of the entire urban region corresponded to the new suburban railway tunnel within the Milan municipal area, which was gradually opened starting in 1997 (Bolocan Goldstein and Bonfantini, 2007; Morandi, 2007). Running from the north-west of the city to the south-east, this new infrastructure enabled the activatation of a new suburban train network that integrated the already existing regional train by contributing to re-directing the urban change process of the urban core towards an urban region perspective. This project led to a first change of scale for the city, recently followed by a new one determined by the new high-speed railway system under development since the 2000s[9] that strengthened the relations among the Milan urban region and other important cities of the Northern Italy macro-region.[10]

The Milan urban region and the socio-spatial consequences of the crisis

The world financial and economic crisis has affected the economic and social, but also spatial and institutional, dynamics of cities within advanced economy countries, in particular in Southern European cities (Knieling and Othengrafen, 2016). This global "contraction" phase started in 2007 with the burst of the speculative property bubble in the US, and it has spread across Europe since 2008 as a financial and a sovereign debt crisis. Being structural and not cyclical, it demands new policies able to overcome the dominant and no longer sustainable development model not only economically, but also socially and environmentally. Accordingly, cities need to promote new, and no longer growth dependent, urban strategies and plans (Rydin, 2013).

As anticipated, whilst the Milan urban region has always been a dynamic area – well integrated with global networks, and characterized by diversified sectoral patterns – from the late 1970s to the 1990s it was affected by a long and complex transition from a mainly, but not exclusively, industrial-based economy to a mainly, but not only, service-based one. This transition – that occurred with limited social costs[11] – enabled Milan to consolidate itself as a gateway city, placed at the eighth position in the worldwide ranking, and at the third position in the European ranking for connectivity (Taylor, 2004). Despite the fragmentation of local businesses – that is one of the main characters of Italian economy – Milan still registered fair economic performances (OECD, 2006). Furthermore, since the beginning of the world crisis, Milan's economic performances have been better than in other Italian cities, for instance, in terms of unemployment rate, growth of new firms, foreign direct investments, or limited decrease of real estate prices (Briata, Di Vita and Pasqui, 2016). Despite the Italian problems of efficiency, competitiveness, but also regulatory quality and control of corruption – for instance, underlined by the World Bank's Worldwide Governance Indicators 2015[12] – it has been favoured by a polyarchy of public and private actors, able to mobilize local resources and to attract external investments, talents, and technologies.

Even through the crisis, Milan and its urban region still represent the most dynamic socio-economic and spatial system in Italy. For instance, in the Mercer's international quality of living ranking,[13] Milan moves from the 46th position in 2015 to the 41st position in 2016 (with London in 39th and Paris in 37th). The entire Milan metropolitan area confirms itself as the main Italian financial and economic hub, and it has been developing as the core of the Italian knowledge, creative, and digital economy[14] with a growing sharing approach (Mariotti, Pacchi and Di Vita, 2017).

Together with Rome – that is the political capital of the country, and one of the religious capitals of the world – Milan confirms itself as one of the two Italian global cities. However, international classifications rank it outside the list of the top 20 worldwide global cities, mainly because of some specific weaknesses related, for instance, to its international political role (Atkearney, 2014), as well to its secondary-level airport system and its urban space quality (UNCTAD, 2015).

Even though Milan has high-level national connections and – according to future completion of above mentioned European corridors – international connections, its airport system is not entirely exploited. This is mainly due to weak national airport policies, which penalize the world competitiveness of

Italian airports. In 2015, the three Milan airports – Malpensa (MXP), Linate (LIN), and Orio al Serio (BGY) (Figure 1.3) – amassed only 36.5 million passengers, whilst the six London airports amassed 156 million passengers, and the three Paris airports amassed 100 million passengers.[15]

From the spatial point of view, the local effects of the recent global economic downturn have determined a frequent downgrade of large real estate projects, which characterized the first service sector urban metamorphosis from the 1980s to the first 2000s in Milan (as in other cities in advanced economy countries). Whilst the crisis penalized an already incomplete metropolis due to a longstanding lack of a broad and shared vision (Bolocan Goldstein and Bonfantini, 2007), austerity measures – introduced in an attempt to alleviate the impact of the crisis itself (such as government policies seeking to reduce budget deficit) – caused additional pressures at local level.[16] Nevertheless, they have stimulated different forms of innovations. On the one hand, besides service rationalization (Fujita, 2013), they emphasized the role of new forms of urban governance (Chapter 6 by Corinna Morandi and Mario Paris), local activation through temporary projects (Chapters 4 and 7 by Antonella Bruzzese and Simonetta Armondi, respectively), and municipal leadership (Chapter 10 by Gabriele Pasqui). On the other hand, they have lent to the growth of innovative services, as well as new hybrid functions and workplaces, which are also favoured by the raising of ICTs (Chapter 5, 8, and 9 by Carolina Pacchi, Stefano Di Vita, and Andrea Rolando, respectively).

Urban change through a new economic base

The supremacy of the Milan economic base on that of other Italian cities has grown since the country unification in the nineteenth century, and it has restated in these last years. On the one hand, the city and its urban region have been less vulnerable to the crisis in comparison with other areas of the Italian territory. On the other, since 2015, they have been driving a post-crisis phase that – even if still weak and uncertain in comparison with urban regions located in other countries and continents[17] – is marking a first discontinuity with the past seven years (Camera di Commercio di Milano, 2016).[18]

Before the global economic crisis, according to the 2006 OECD Territorial Review, Milan is the core of a wider and very productive urban region[19] that corresponds to the richest Italian area, and remains one of the top-ranked OECD urban agglomerations, making a fundamental contribution to the entire country's competitiveness. However, this wide spatial and productive platform is now challenged to switch into an international creative service hub, intimately linked with its vibrant manufacturing background. Therefore, in order to maintain its Southern European leading role, Milan needs to upgrade high-level business services, as well as to invest in both its traditional assets and innovation. Indeed, whilst the international competitions among cities is increasingly strong, in the last years the city lost part of its historical attractiveness, so that it risks decreasing its rank within the world's most productive regions and most competitive non capital regions.

This is also due to a local governance fragmentation and the consequent difficulties for local actors in building a broad and shared urban vision, able to orient public policies and address very complicated issues from mobility, to liveability and innovation (OECD, 2006). This vision – dealing with the entire urban region, which the urban core is now inextricably connected to – could provide a common scenario, which the single projects, frequently supported by specific European or national funds, should refer to.

After the breaking out of the world crisis, the recent success of the Expo 2015[20] has contributed to reconsolidating the local and international attractiveness of the city, as well as its positive image, for instance catalysing and accelerating several already ongoing trends:

• the Milan affirmation as a tourist destination (not only for business, but also for leisure);[21]
• the renewal of the city's image, now rebranded among the most attractive European cities, such as Barcelona, London, or Paris;
• the acceleration in the implementation of flagship and infrastructural projects.

This ongoing metamorphosis of the urban economic base deals with a Milan transition from city exclusively oriented to production, finance, and business tourism, to urban region also characterized by several leisure opportunities. Accordingly – besides the 2015 World's Fair (integrated by a new urban event platform called *Expo in Città*,[22] still operating) and the 2016 Triennale International Exhibition (located in the historical Triennale *Palazzo dell'Arte* and in other sites of the Milan urban core[23]) – art and cultural events are growing in several facilities and city districts (Figure 1.8). On the one hand, the new most important and attractive art and cultural centres are the ones of the Prada Foundation and the Feltrinelli Foundation, together with new museums such as the *Museo del Novecento* and the *MUDEC*[24] (by reusing former industrial buildings or vacant spaces).[25] On the other, the most important and attractive Milan districts – also involved by yearly events such as *Design Week* and *Fashion Week* (widespread in the city) – are *Brera, Isola-Porta Garibaldi-Porta Nuova, Porta Genova-Tortona, Porta Romana*, the so-called *Quadrilatero*, or *Ventura-Lambrate*, just to mention the most famous (Bolocan Goldstein, 2009; Bruzzese and Tamini, 2014; Bruzzese, 2015).

Together with new opportunities, and even through a post-crisis restart and the Expo success, Milan should still invest on its advanced functions and productions in order to stimulate the innovation of its urban region, but also drive the development of the whole country, and maintain its rank within other important global cities. From specialized productions of its firms (such as furniture, electric equipment, mechanical engineering),[26] to ICTs and clusters of knowledge-intensive activities (such as biotechnology, business services, creative industries),[27] up to new relationships between private and public companies, universities, and research institutions[28] (OECD, 2006).

The spatial and socio-economic change of Milan is a challenging and intriguing example of trans-scalar dynamics and production innovations. It displays a representation of the relationships between late capitalism and work in the aftermath of the 2008 economic crisis, for which the chapters of this books offer an interpretation. From certain aspects, the Milan urban region – into the wider Northern Italy macro-area – recalls the situation of highly developed global city-regions in the world. At the same time – at the urban region scale – the city seems to highlight a pronounced metamorphosis connected with neo-manufacturing perspective and the role of innovation in urban contexts (Armondi and Bolocan Goldstein, 2015). It concerns the combination between:

- some local and traditional economies related to *Made in Italy* in a diffused system of small and artisan firms, scattered in different urban region districts (i.e., fashion, design, furniture) linked with the global giant brands;
- the presence of some specialized services (i.e. health, higher education and research, finance) and productions (i.e., mechanic, mechatronics, chemical and pharmaceutical, logistics, aviation, silk, plastic, taps) (Centro Studi PIM, 2016).

This production combination of new craftsmanship, advanced goods, and innovative services seems to encourage the creation of a new generation of workers (in the production of goods, services, and of value), but also of innovative workplaces such as co-working spaces, makerspaces, and other hybrid spaces[29] (Figure 1.8). Italy remains an important advanced manufacturing country in relation not only to peculiar productions of *Made in Italy*, but also to automation, robotics, chemical, and rubber-plastic productions. However, whilst the current challenge is digital manufacturing – about which there are several potentials, but also criticalities, in comparison with other industrial countries (Calabrò, 2015; Centro Studi

PIM, 2016) – Milan has taken it. According to recent analyses of the city, there are at least three main aspects which are able to boost the growth of knowledge and creative economy in the densest urban core of the wider Milan urban region:

• Milan is often depicted as "self-governing city", because the role of private actors (profit and non-profit), and of higher education and cultural institutions has always been as important as that of local authorities in setting the urban agenda and in implementing urban projects. For this reason, bottom up innovative initiatives, in particular in business, as well as in social and cultural sectors, are very frequent.

• Milan shows, at the same time, an increasing demand and supply of economic and social innovations, because of growing knowledge exchanges with local universities, cooperation with local advanced firms, and significant spatial support by specific local policies promoted by the City Council.[30] Compared with other international urban contexts, and with other Italian cities, the Milan urban region has the higher number of employees in innovative sectors.[31] Therefore, Milan seems to have reacted to the current economic downturn not only by exploiting its traditional economic and social strengths (i.e., high level of entrepreneurship and social cooperation), but also by favouring the rise of a sharing economy and society. That is, the mainly spontaneous growth of new, flexible, and cheaper working spaces, where new activities are promoted by sharing spaces, exchanging expertise and, consequently, reducing costs (Mariotti, Pacchi and Di Vita, 2017).

The new urban plan – approved by the Milan Municipality in 2012 – includes innovative workplaces (such as incubators, co-working spaces, makerspaces) within the system of city services in order to facilitate their development. At the same time, it identifies not only large areas for the development of future big projects, but also entire districts to be subject to renovation (Di Vita, 2017a).

The Milan urban region is interwoven with other urban nodes of the Northern Italy city-region, as well as other European and world cities. For instance, through the Milan Food Policy Pact, promoted on the occasion of the Expo 2015, or the links with London, from the current Milan bid to host the European Medicines Agency[32] (that is going to leave the post-Brexit UK), to the 2017 fusion between the Italian Stock Exchange and the London Stock Exchange.[33] Concerning the above mentioned Milan resilience in the transition from old manufacturing (and traditional services) to advanced services (and new manufacturing), a core role has been played by universities as both producers of knowledge-based urban assets, and developers contributing to important large-scale redevelopment projects in brownfields (Balducci, Cognetti and Fedeli, 2010). Even though a low level of cooperation between different academic institutions, and a not completely successful coordination by public actors (e.g., the Lombardy Regional Government and the Milan Municipality), Milan universities have made an important contribution to anti-cyclical initiatives and to economic performances of the urban region, also through the cooperation with public institutions (Briata, Di Vita and Pasqui, 2016). Furthermore, Milan universities have a role in the face of the crisis, for instance by promoting an articulated system of actions:

• the development of real estate initiatives in a period of severe contraction for the real estate market;
• the supply of innovative services for both students and other urban populations;
• the promotion of innovative entrepreneurial activities;
• a growing role in the organization and management of larger and smaller events.

For instance, Milan universities are now involved within the ongoing, but still uncertain, implementation of the proposals for the post-event reuse of the Expo site.[34]

For sure, the 2015 World's Fair has been an occasion for innovation and improvement of city services and infrastructures, beginning with the new technological endowment of both the event site and the Milan urban region.[35] Nevertheless, besides the event, even the Department for Innovation, Economic Development and Universities of the Milan Municipality has been investing in technological innovation together with social inclusion, with positive effects in terms of knowledge economy's growth. For instance, the approval of the Milan Smart City Guidelines (May 2014) and the Milan Sharing City Guidelines (December 2014) highlight the importance of ICTs as engines of urban change, and the meaning of cooperation and sharing economy for future urban development (Gascó, Trivellato and Cavenago, 2015; Armondi and Bruzzese, 2017). Even though all these activities still seem weak in comparison with other European cities, they are innovative from the methodological point of view. Furthermore, they are opportunities for a socio-economic renovation, even though they need a further implementation and consolidation through a change of scale, from the Municipal level to (at least) the new Metropolitan City (Di Vita, 2017b), up to the urban region.

Accordingly, to the transcalarity of the Milan spatial and socio-economic dynamics that make it similar to other world cities (playing as international actors), one of the main challenges for its future urban policies should be the strengthening of a necessary sensitivity to both local and supra-local relations; that is, going beyond the scales of both local and national authorities (Dierwechter, 2017; Herrschel and Newman, 2017).

Conclusion

Milan opens up to new geographies of industrialization and territorial development changing its economic base. Nonetheless, today, economies spread wide across territories. In fact, talking about regional or urban (Brenner and Schmid, 2015), administrative borders of territories are increasingly blurred, and production activities are far more de-located than in the past. Hence, spatial and socio-economic dynamics transverse boundaries. Consequently, at the present moment, local authorities such as the Region, or the Metropolitan City, solely from an administrative point of view, have only limited impact on urban change.

Therefore, on the one hand, it is possible to conclude that, despite the financial crisis and the austerity measures, the polyarchic local governance still remains one of the key drivers for the prosecution of the collective interest and the innovation in productive systems. On the other hand, as the following images show, urban change is strictly linked with complex, contested, and contradictory relations between places, scales, networks, and related administrative organizations. It is also on these bases that future urban and regional policies need to be reorganized.

Notes

1 See Chapter 2.
2 The Metropolitan City is a new government tier defined in April 2014 by the Italian National Law n. 56 in substitution of the former Province, and officially established in January 2015. For a critical perspective on the Italian notion of metropolitan city see Armondi (2017).
3 That comprehends all the administrative regions of Northern Italy, thus including the highly urbanized Po Valley.
4 For instance, 1 per cent in 2004–2007.
5 See Chapters 7, 8, and 9.
6 See Chapter 7.
7 See Chapter 2.
8 See Chapter 10.
9 See Chapter 10.
10 The new high-speed railway lines Milan-Turin (partially opened in 2006 and completed in 2009), Milan-Bologna (opened in 2008), and Milan-Brescia (opened in 2016).

11 See also Chapter 2.

12 Available at www.govindicators.org/.

13 Available at www.imercer.com/content/mobility/quality-of-living-city-rankings. html Accessed December 2016.

14 For instance, whilst in Germany medium-tech makes up 8.2 per cent of the total employment, and in Italy as a whole this sector is at 4.9 per cent, in Milan and in Lombardy it is 7.7 per cent, half a point below the German figure (Assolombarda, 2015). Furthermore, in Milan 16.2 per cent of workers are employed in manufacturing (including fashion and food, engineering and chemistry), 7.2 per cent in information and communication services, 10.8 per cent in professional scientific and technical activities, and 6.3 per cent in finance.

15 According to Eurostat, the 2015 top airports of the European Union are: 1. London Heathrow (75 million passengers); 2. Paris Charles des Gaulle (65.7 million passengers); 3. Frankfurt (60.9 million passengers); 4. Amsterdam Schipol (58.2 million passengers); 5. Madrid Barajas (46.3 million passengers); 6. Munich (40.9 million passengers); 7. London Gatwick (40.3 million passengers); 8. Rome Fiumicino (40.2 million passengers); 9. Barcelona El Prat (39.4 million passengers); 10. Paris Orly (29.7 million passengers). The main Milan Malpensa airport is only 22 (with 18.5 million passengers) (source: Eurostat).

16 See Chapter 10.

17 In 2015 the Italian GDP grew by +0.8 per cent, while the Euro area GDP grew by +1.6 per cent, and the world GDP grew by +3.1 per cent (Camera di Commercio di Milano, 2016).

18 In 2015 the Italian GDP grew by +0.8 per cent, while the Milan Metropolitan City GDP grew by +1.2 per cent. In particular, in Milan, the industrial production grew by +0.8 per cent, the manufacturing craftsmanship grew by +2.9 per cent, the retail grew by 2.8 per cent, and the service sector grew by +2.5 per cent. At the same time, the employment grew by +2.1 per cent, and the (still high) young unemployment rate was 22 per cent in comparison with the 30 per cent at the national level (Camera di Commercio di Milano, 2016).

19 According to the OECD Territorial Review, besides the area of the current Milan Metropolitan City, the Milan urban region includes the area of eight current Italian provinces. Seven are in Lombardy (such as Bergamo, Como, Lecco, Lodi, Monza e Brianza, Pavia, Varese), and one is in Piedmont (such as Novara) (OECD, 2006).

20 According to recent data, the Expo produced new businesses for 31.6 billion €, 242,000 new jobs, and the foundation or consolidation of more than 10,000 firms (Camera di Commercio, 2016).

21 The tourist arrivals grew from 5.6 million in 2010 to 7.3 million in 2015 (Camera di Commercio, 2016).

22 Available at it.expoincitta.com.

23 Such as the *Fabbrica del Vapore, Hangar Bicocca, Politecnico di Milano* campuses, *IULM* campus, *MUDEC, Museo della Scienza e della Tecnologia, BASE, Palazzo della Permanente,* Expo site, and *Museo Diocesano,* in Milan, as well as the *Villa Reale,* in Monza (source: www.arte.it/calendario-arte/milano/ mostra-xxi-esposizione-internazionale-della-triennale-di-milano-21st-century-design-after-design-20965).

24 MUDEC stands for *MUseo DElle Culture.*

25 See Chapters 6, 8, and 9.
26 See Chapters 3 and 10.
27 See Chapters 4 and 5.
28 See Chapter 8.
29 See Chapter 5.
30 Specifically, the 2011–2016 Municipal Administration provided economic support to private initiatives aimed at developing co-working spaces and makerspaces, and it has directly invested in incubators. In particular, since 2013, economic incentives have been made available to favour the proliferation of mainly spontaneous new workplaces; that is, to support activities of co-workers and makers, and to improve the physical quality of new working spaces registered in a qualified list in relation to requirements specifically established (Armondi and Bruzzese, 2017, Di Vita, 2017a).
31 Source: Atlas of Post-Metropolitan Territories (available at www.postmetropoli. it/atlante/).
32 See Chapter 2.
33 That formed the new London Stock Exchange Group.
34 See Chapter 8.
35 From the Expo Smart City project for the exhibition area, to the E015 Digital Ecosystem for the entire urban region (Bruzzese and Di Vita, 2016).

References

Armondi, S. (2015). Spazio urbano e nuove geografie della produzione: Una lettura internazionale. *Imprese & Città*, 8, pp. 56–62.
Armondi, S. (2017). State rescaling and new metropolitan space in the age of austerity: Evidence from Italy. *Geoforum*, 81, pp. 174–179.
Armondi, S. and Bolocan Goldstein, M. (2015). Spazio urbano e nuove geografie della produzione: una riflessione a partire da Milano. In: AA.VV, ed., *Italian urbanists conference: Italia 45–45. Radici, condizioni, prospettive*. Roma-Milano: Planum Publisher, pp. 40–52.
Armondi, S. and Bruzzese, A. (2017). Contemporary productions and urban change. *Journal of Urban Technology*, 24:3. Available online: http://www.tandfonline. com/doi/full/10.1080/10630732.2017.1311567
Assolombarda. (2015). *Il lavoro a Milano*. Milano: Assolombarda.
Atkearney. (2014). *Global cities, present and future*. Available at: www. atkearney.com/latest-article/-/asset_publisher/lON5IOfbQl6C/content/ global-cities-present-and-future-gci-2014/10192.
Balducci, A., Cognetti, F. and Fedeli, V. eds. (2010). *Milano. La città degli Studi, Storia, geografia e politiche delle università milanesi*. Milano: Abitare Segesta.
Balducci, A., Fedeli, V. and Pasqui, G. eds. (2011). *Strategic planning for contemporary urban regions*. Aldershot: Ashgate.
Bolocan Goldstein, M. (2009). *Geografie milanesi*. Santarcangelo di Romagna: Maggioli.
Bolocan Goldstein, M. and Bonfantini, B. eds. (2007). *Milano incompiuta*. Milano: Franco Angeli.

Brenner, N. and Schmid, C. (2015). Towards a new epistemology of the urban. *City*, 19(2–3), pp. 151–182.

Briata, P., Di Vita, S. and Pasqui, G. (2016). *Urban policy and responses to the crisis: The role of academic and research institutions in Milan.* Paper presented at the *EURA Conference*.

Bruzzese, A. (2015). *Addensamenti creativi, trasformazioni urbane e Fuorisalone.* Santarcangelo di Romagna: Maggioli.

Bruzzese, A. and Di Vita, S. eds. (2016). Expo 2015 and its Legacies. *Territorio*, 77, pp. 67–109.

Bruzzese, A. and Tamini, L. (2014). *Servizi commerciali e prodizioni creative: Sei itinerari nella Milano che cambia.* Milano: Mondadori.

Calabrò, A. (2015). *La morale del tornio: Cultura d'impresa per lo sviluppo.* Milano: Università Bocconi.

Camera di Commercio di Milano. (2016). *Milano produttiva 2016.* Milano: Bruno Mondadori.

Centro Studi PIM. (2016). Spazialità metropolitane: Economia, società e territorio. *Argomenti e Contributi*, 15, Special Issue.

Cucca, R. and Ranci, C. eds. (2017). *Unequal cities: The challenge of post-industrial transition in times of austerity.* London, New York: Routledge.

Dente, B., Bobbio, L. and Spada A. (2005). Government or governance of urban innovation? A tale of two cities, *Disp, The Planning Review*, 162, pp. 41–53.

Di Vita, S. (2017a). I makerspace di Milano: Quali politiche pubbliche? In: M. D'Ovidio and C. Rabbiosi, eds., *Makers e città. La rivoluzione si fa con al stampante 3D?* Milano: Feltrinelli (in press).

Di Vita, S. (2017b). Le politiche pubbliche di Milano sui makerspace: Quali effetti? Quali prospettive? In: M. D'Ovidio and C. Rabbiosi, eds., *Makers e città: La rivoluzione si fa con al stampante 3D?* Milano: Feltrinelli (in press).

Dierwechter, Y. (2017). *Urban sustainability through smart growth.* Cham: Springer.

Fujita, K. (2013). *Cities and crisis. New critical urban theory.* London: Sage.

Gascó, M., Trivellato, B. and Cavenago, D. (2015). How do Southern European cities foster innovation? Lessons from the experience of the smart city approaches of Barcelona and Milan. In: J.R. Gill, T. Garcia, A. Pardo and T. Nam, eds., *Smarter as the new urban agenda: A comprehensive view of the 21st century city.* Cham (Switzerland): Springer, pp. 191–206.

Gualini, E. (2003). The region of Milan. In: W. Salet, A. Thornley and A. Kreukels, eds., *Metropolitan Governance and Spatial Planning.* London-New York: Spon Press.

Herrschel, T. and Newman, P. (2017). *Cities as international actors: Urban and regional governance beyond the nation state.* London: Palgrave MacMillan.

Knieling, J. and Othengrafen, F. eds. (2016). *Cities in crisis.* Abingdon: Routledge.

Mariotti, I., Pacchi, C. and Di Vita, S. (2017). Coworking spaces in Milan: ICTs, proximity, and urban effects. *Journal of Urban Technology*, 24:3. Available online: http://www.tandfonline.com/doi/full/10.1080/10630732.2017.1311556.

Morandi, C. (2007). *Milan: The great urban transformation.* Venezia: Marsilio.

OECD. (2006). *OECD territorial reviews. Milan, Italy.* Paris: OECD Publishing.

Perulli, P. (2014). Milan in the age of global contract. *Glocalism: Journal of Culture, Politics and Innovation*, 3, Globus et Locus. Available at: www.glocalism journal.net.

Perulli P. (2016). *The urban contract: Community, Governance and Capitalism.* London: Routledge.

Perulli, P., and Pichierri, A. (2010). *La crisi italiana nel mondo globale. Economia e società del Nord.* Torino: Einaudi.

Rydin, Y. (2013). *The future of planning: Beyond growth dependence.* Bristol: University of Bristol Policy Press.

Scott, A.J., ed. (2001). *Global city-regions: Trends, theory, policy.* Oxford: Oxford University Press.

Taylor, P. (2004). *World city networks: A global urban analysis.* London, New York: Routledge.

UNCTAD. (2015). *United nations conference on trade and development world investment.* New York, Geneve: Report, United Nations.

An atlas of the Milan change and networks

(maps elaborated by Angelo Armentano, Centro Studi PIM)

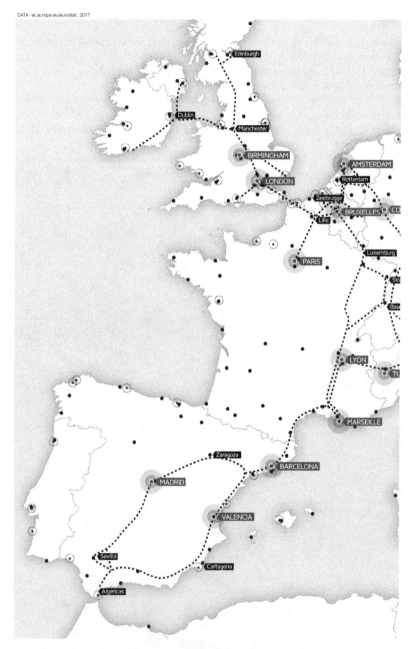

Figure 1.1 The Milan urban region in the European space

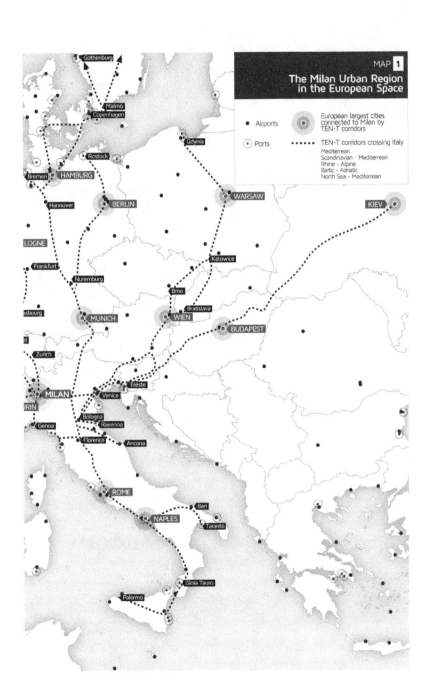

MAP 1

The Milan Urban Region in the European Space

● Airports

⊙ Ports

European largest cities connected to Milan by TEN-T corridors

········· TEN-T corridors crossing Italy
Mediterrean
Scandinavian – Mediterrean
Rhine – Alpine
Baltic – Adriatic
North Sea – Mediterrean

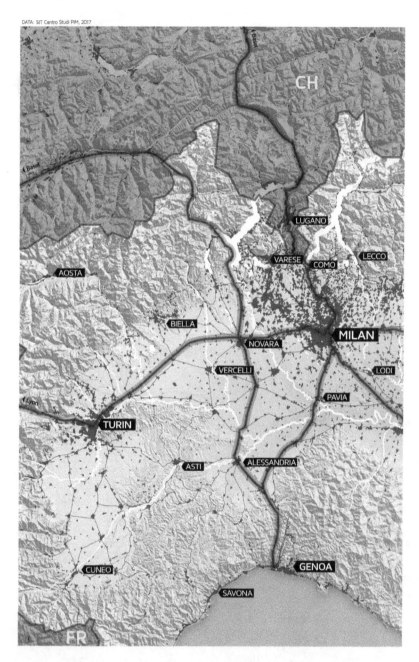

Figure 1.2 The Milan urban region within the Northern Italy city region

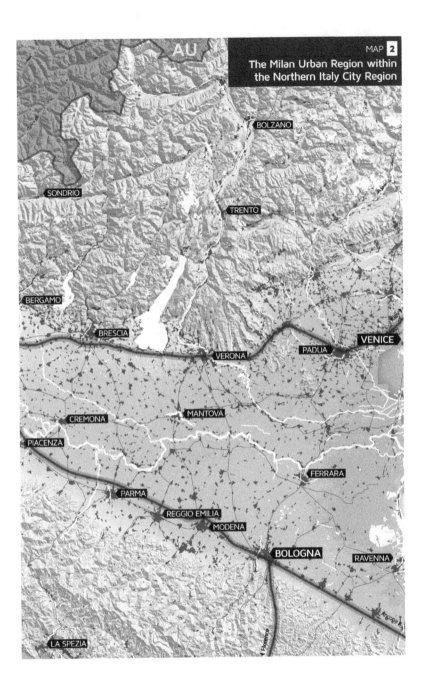

MAP 2

The Milan Urban Region within
the Northern Italy City Region

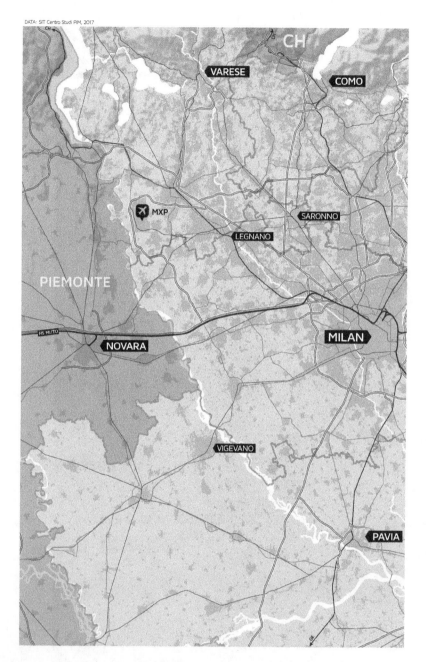

Figure 1.3 The Milan urban region: physical components

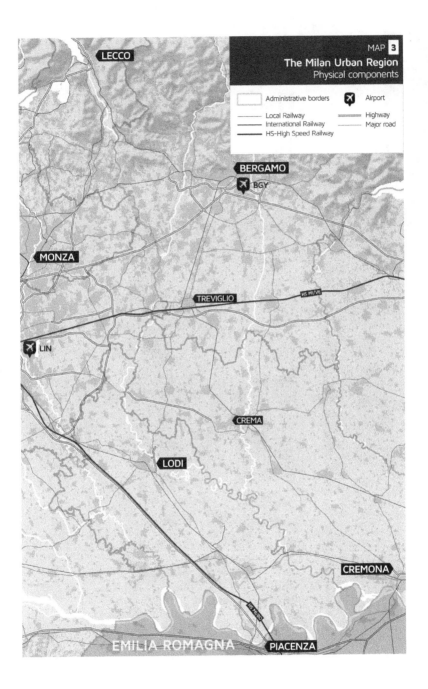

MAP **3**
The Milan Urban Region
Physical components

Administrative borders
Local Railway
International Railway
HS-High Speed Railway
Airport
Highway
Major road

LECCO

BERGAMO
BGY

MONZA

TREVIGLIO
HS MI/VE

LIN

CREMA

LODI

CREMONA

EMILIA ROMAGNA
HS MI/BO
PIACENZA

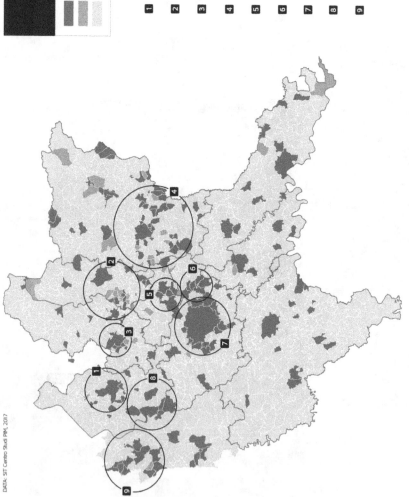

MAP **4**

The Milan Urban Region
Economic framework

Central municipalities
Second level municipalities
Residential municipalities

FUNCTIONS

1 AGGREGATION OF VARESE
public function and mechanical

2 AGGREGATION OF LECCO
mechanical

3 AGGREGATION OF COMO
public function and silk district

4 AGGREGATION OF BERGAMO
mechanical and plastics

5 AGGREGATION OF MONZA
public function and electromechanical

6 EAST MILAN
chemical, pharmaceutical and logistics

7 MILAN
advanced service sector

8 MALPENSA AREA
aviation and logistics

9 NORTH EAST PIEDMONT
district of taps

Figure 1.4 The Milan urban region: economic framework

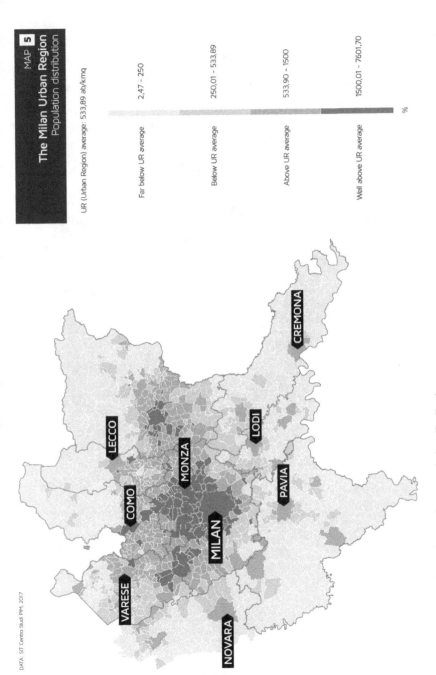

DATA: SIT Centro Studi PIM, 2017

MAP **5**

The Milan Urban Region
Population distribution

UR (Urban Region) average: 533,89 ab/kmq

Far below UR average   2,47 – 250

Below UR average   250,01 – 533,89

Above UR average   533,90 – 1500

Well above UR average   1500,01 – 7601,70

%

CREMONA

LECCO

MONZA

LODI

COMO

PAVIA

MILAN

VARESE

NOVARA

Figure 1.5 The Milan urban region: population distribution

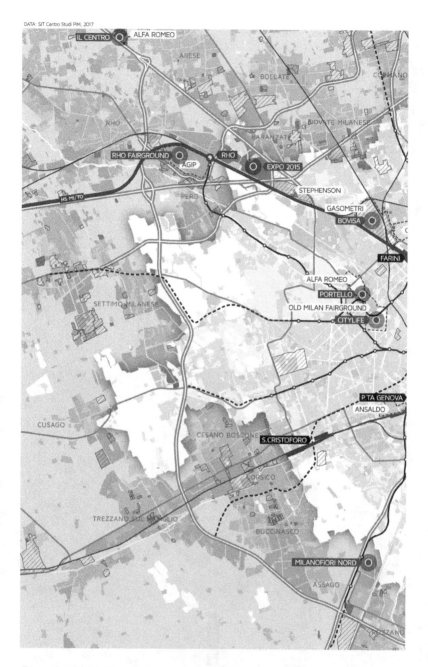

Figure 1.6 The Milan urban core: main urban change projects

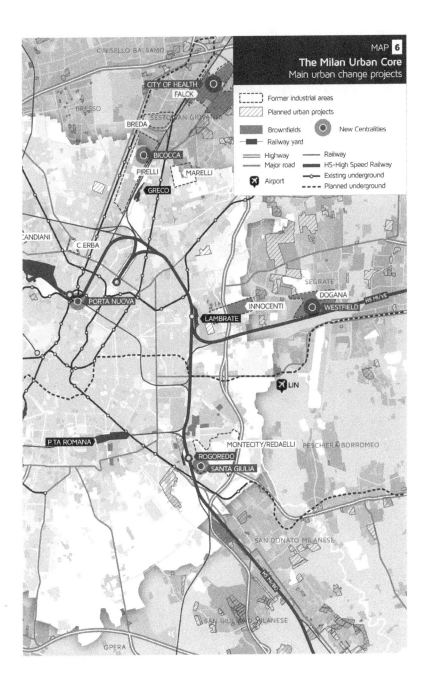

CINISELLO BALSAMO

CITY OF HEALTH

FALCK

BRESSO

SESTO SAN GIOVANNI

BREDA

BICOCCA

PIRELLI

MARELLI

GRECO

CANDIANI

C.ERBA

PORTA NUOVA

SEGRATE

DOGANA

INNOCENTI

WESTFIELD

HS MI/VE

LAMBRATE

LIN

P.TA ROMANA

MONTECITY/REDAELLI

PESCHIERA BORROMEO

ROGOREDO

SANTA GIULIA

SAN DONATO MILANESE

HS MI/BO

SAN GIULIANO MILANESE

OPERA

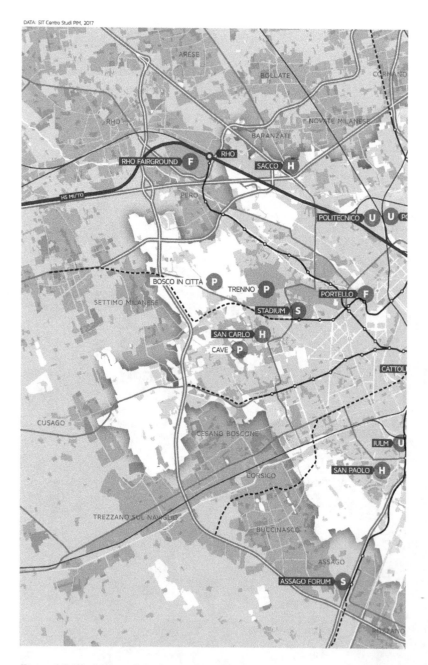

Figure 1.7 The Milan urban core: trans-scalar networks

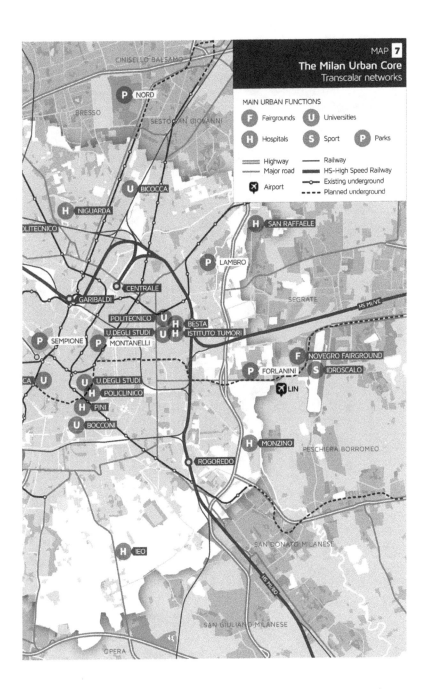

MAP 7
The Milan Urban Core
Transcalar networks

MAIN URBAN FUNCTIONS

F Fairgrounds   U Universities
H Hospitals   S Sport   P Parks

Highway   Railway
Major road   HS-High Speed Railway
Airport   Existing underground
                 Planned underground

NORD
BRESSO
CINISELLO BALSAMO
SESTO SAN GIOVANNI
BICOCCA
NIGUARDA
POLITECNICO
SAN RAFFAELE
LAMBRO
CENTRALE
GARIBALDI
SEGRATE
HS MI/VE
POLITECNICO
U.DEGLI STUDI
SEMPIONE
MONTANELLI
BESTA
ISTITUTO TUMORI
NOVEGRO FAIRGROUND
F
IDROSCALO
FORLANINI
U.DEGLI STUDI
POLICLINICO
LIN
PINI
BOCCONI
MONZINO
PESCHIERA BORROMEO
ROGOREDO
SAN DONATO MILANESE
IEO
HS MI/BO
SAN GIULIANO MILANESE
OPERA

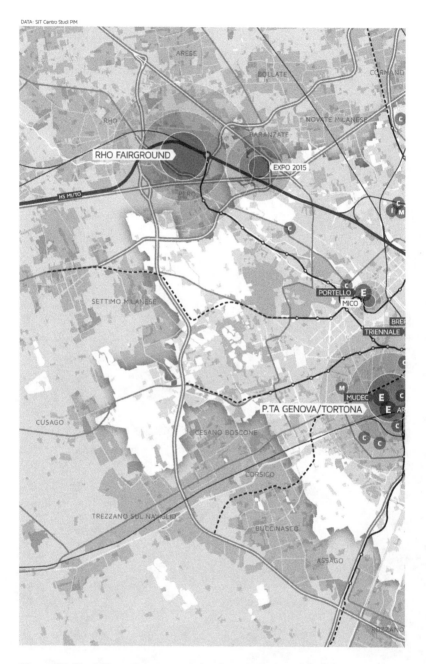

Figure 1.8 The Milan urban core: creative, knowledge-based, and sharing economy

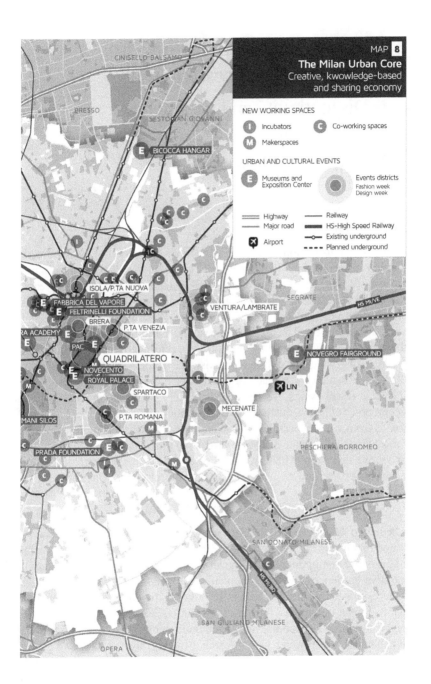

MAP **8**

The Milan Urban Core
Creative, kwowledge-based
and sharing economy

NEW WORKING SPACES

I Incubators   **C** Co-working spaces

M Makerspaces

URBAN AND CULTURAL EVENTS

E Museums and
Exposition Center

Events districts
Fashion week
Design week

Highway   Railway

Major road   HS-High Speed Railway

Airport   Existing underground

Planned underground

CINISELLO BALSAMO

BRESSO

SESTO SAN GIOVANNI

E BICOCCA HANGAR

ISOLA/P.TA NUOVA

FABBRICA DEL VAPORE

FELTRINELLI FOUNDATION

BRERA

P.TA VENEZIA

RA ACADEMY

PAC

QUADRILATERO

NOVECENTO

ROYAL PALACE

SPARTACO

MANI SILOS

P.TA ROMANA

PRADA FOUNDATION

VENTURA/LAMBRATE

SEGRATE

HS MI/VE

E NOVEGRO FAIRGROUND

LIN

MECENATE

PESCHIERA BORROMEO

SAN DONATO MILANESE

HS MI/BO

SAN GIULIANO MILANESE

OPERA

2 Urban regionalization and metropolitan resurgence

Discontinuity and persistence of a spatial dialectic

Matteo Bolocan Goldstein

Introduction

Every urban formation manifests a peculiar trajectory of development through space and time. In the words of Peter Taylor, we might say, a peculiar way of being an "extraordinary city" (Taylor, 2013).[1] In recent years, Milan has increased its self-perception of being a metropolitan reality. This is due to two distinct facts: first, the success of the Expo 2015 event, and second, a complicated institutional measure – the so called *Delrio* law, from the name of the Minister who promoted the reform concerning local powers in 2014 – which established the existence of the metropolitan authority ("Metropolitan city") in place of the former Province. Without disregarding these recent events, we are more interested in considering the multiple geographies of Milan and the spatial implications of certain socio-economic trends from a wider perspective. Geographical dimensions represent a significant "stake" in any discourse around the city and its own evolution. When we talk about Milan, what we often take as the geographical reference is not clear, and the urban reality remains unspecified, or implicit.

Geographical dimensions and inherent spatiality

The *Milan Municipality* is a relatively small reality and spatially concentrated (about 1.3 million inhabitants across 180 km², less than 10 per cent of the entire metropolitan area); the *metropolitan context*, within the administrative borders of the "Metropolitan city", consists of 134 municipalities (over 3 million inhabitants across 1575 km²); the *enlarged urban region*, defined in an important "Territorial review" (OECD, 2006), encompassing eight provinces surrounding the "Metropolitan city" (more than 8 million inhabitants).[2] Finally, in recent research, Milan is now regarded as a *global city-region* involving the whole of Northern Italy (Figure 1.1, Figure 1.2, Figure 1.3), one of the most important continental macro regions (Bolocan

Goldstein and Puttilli, 2011). However, if such plural geographical horizons are mainly concentrated on multiscalar territorial entities, it is also significant to consider how, under the cover of urban morphologies "on the ground", a variety of flows and functional relationships are characterized by the inherent spatiality, connecting the Milan node to an ever expanding worldwide dimension.

From this point of view, the treatment of the geographies of Milan has to take into consideration interdependent phenomena, those concerning territorial/settlement dynamics, and also reticular/functional projections. On the basis of this dual perspective Milan is extremely difficult to describe, according to international standard patterns – *world city*, *metropolitan region*, *global city*, *global city-region*, and so on – due to the frequent lack of convergence between this dual, territorial/functional, spatial logic. Provisionally, Milan could be considered as a dynamic second ranked *world city* and, simultaneously it represents the main driver supporting a wider Northern macro-region (from Turin to Bologna and Trieste).[3] At the same time, it has been observed as an active node, part of the world city network (Taylor, 2004). Such geographical complexity doesn't only apply to the current "late-modern" phase, but represents a geo-historical trait of Milan and its regional background. The main point that needs emphasizing is primarily the presence of this geo-historical dialectic as an original feature of Milan's dynamism, "traversing" multiple geographical scales.

Historically, on the "urban scale", the nineteenth-century affair of the "Corpi Santi" (Holy Bodies)[4] occurred when Milan embedded several autonomous settlements surrounding the city with a distinct fiscal regime, considered unfavourable by the City government. In another context, which was characterized by the intensive urbanization of the Second Post-war period, on the "metropolitan area scale", we can also note the troubled story of the inter-municipality plan and the territorial dispute between the City of Milan and several surrounding municipalities. A final example, on the "macro-region scale", is the contemporary rivalry between Milan and Turin concerning the future of the annual Book Fair. These are just a few examples – amongst others – to illustrate certain decisive issues reflecting territorial/spatial dialectics in their historical and social specificity. It is in this problematic context that we will consider the significant role of Milan throughout the twentieth century up to the present day.

Focusing on the city's socio-economic role over its long period of growth, it is necessary to observe the intricate linkage between territoriality and public policy. In the final section of this chapter, we will turn our attention to the recent period, so marked by the effects of worldwide economic and spatial "contraction".

Milan's primacy in the "long" twentieth century: the era of growth

A geo-historical premise for a multi-sectorial original city

The primacy of Milan dates back to the late Middles Ages and the same ancient toponym of *Mediolanum* would seem to refer to both the natural geographical features – an area of large agricultural farm activity coinciding with three distinct rivers the Olona, Seveso, and Lambro – and to its geostrategic position in the centre of the fertile Padana Valley, along the Po river basin. This simple reference allows us to understand the geographical complexity of the regional/urban relationships and to interpret the Milanese reality observing the city from the outside, from the point of view of a wider macro region. In this regard, it is important to consider that, between the eighteenth and nineteenth centuries, the first phase of Italian industrialization developed predominantly in the foothills of the Northern regions. It was characterized by diffused small peasant landownerships and by share-cropping which featured lower labour productivity (as a consequence of a higher labour/land ratio). Such socio-economic factors affected farms in these areas, which suffered competition from farms in the lower plain, which for a long period had seen heavy investment in land reclamation and canalization works.

The capitalistic development of agriculture in the lower irrigated plain (with larger country properties, specific organization of labour and market-production not only for self-consumption) represents the general conditions of the different economic trajectory in the higher dry plain. For these reasons too, the first phase of the industrialization process was based on a strong fragmentation of domestic work, a significant agriculture/manufacturing production interdependency, and a type of social and spatial city-countryside complementarity.

This brief geo-historical overview shows how the pre-eminent position of Milan depends on an initial *geographical dominance*, as a city situated between the higher and lower plain, and an increasing *territorial centrality* as a communication and transport crossroad. As a consequence, Milan has consolidated its image as a *midland*, due to its strategic positioning within a concentric geographical configuration of various major towns.

Within this regional framework, the "industrial take off" of the city occurred with a certain amount of delay, compared to other European industrial cities, at the end of the nineteenth century, during the "long epoch" of the industrial era.[5] In the period following national unification (1861), Milan experienced an important period of urban renewal and in particular during the 1880s its profile became that of a true "industrial city". Between

1890 and 1915, a growing population (from 368,000 to 665,000 inhabitants, +81 per cent) and the effect of industrial employment (in 1909 the Province of Milan represented almost 20 per cent of the entire Italian industrial occupation) are the most evident signs of a new era.

It is significant to note an important aspect regarding the local political-economy orientation which made Milan a model of the so called Municipal Socialism, while simultaneously affirming the city as a strong industrial base. This phenomenon reinforced the international profile of *Milan as a European city* which has become a constant reference up to the present day. Based on these factors, Milan's strong points at the turn of the nineteenth and twentieth centuries combine a historical profile as a commercial hub and its new manufacturing role. This included the early introduction of heavy industry, the "beginning of the Fordist fanfare" observed by Antonio Gramsci, although still far from an *"Americanist* mentality" (Gramsci, 1975). The geographical symbol of this industrial organization of urban economies during the *long twentieth century* was initially the *Industrial Triangle* (Milan-Turin-Genoa), a clear image which exemplifies the "large city/big company" nexus (Figure 1.2), and its role as a driving force behind the whole economy. The end of this long industrial era (the conclusion of this epoch as generally identified by Charles Mayer between the 1960s–1980s) corresponds to the abandonment of a city-centred geography of development in favour of the Northern Italy macro-regional formation, in which the same Milanese urban region can be considered as a dominant geographical section of the wider Padana plain extending from the West (Turin) to the East (Bologna, Venice, and Trieste).

Taking into account these geographical reconfigurations of Milan's role in different scenarios, we can now focus on analysing the Second Post-war period consisting of two distinct, only partially overlapping, spread socio-economic and spatial cycles. The first, covering the period between the 1950s up to the 1970s, can be summarized applying the image of "bigness", starting from the expanding dimensions of the city supported by an intense industrialization process. The second cycle occurs during the 1970s and continues until the early 1990s reflected by the general urban crisis throughout the 1970s as seen through the wider trend of a spreading territorial development. Two cycles, significantly different in terms of growth rates, economic-sectorial composition and geographical distribution of activities, but both characterized by the combination of intense material processes and influent territorial images: desirable images, as well as concrete realities.

Urban concentration, or the myth of spatial equilibrium

The urban polarization of the development process characterized the Republican phase until the late 1960s. The so-called Italian "economic Miracle"

(1953/1963) was driven by the huge demographic concentration in Northern cities of the country. This was a highly polarized territorial development where the main industrial cities – with Milan taking a leading role – represented a sort of immense "magnet", an actual force field engendered by the surrounding contexts situated along the main communication routes.

It is precisely this period of more intense growth that determined increasing territorial differences at various scales within the country, and this phenomenon involved the whole "Italy of the Miracle", as well as internal Milan/Lombardy spatial relationships. To deal with such unequal territorial trends – South/North historical macro variances, but also metropolitan and regional spatial inequalities – public policies of that period targeted a generalized rebalance of the territorial dynamic. This was achieved by means of "poles of development" and new infrastructure investment in Southern Italy, but also with public interventions and economic programming in the North. This was the case in the Milan and Lombardy region during the 1960s, where the Milanese Inter-municipality experimental plan (PIM) and the experience of the *Regional committee for the economic programming* (CRPE) influenced the local decision-making process.[6] It is a phase in which the territory was seen as "passive support" for the capitalistic accumulation of the country. A self-propelling accumulation in the North-West regions of the "industrial triangle", in contrast to top down intervention across the rest of Italy, in particular in the Southern regions. Nevertheless, the goal of "spatial equilibrium" that informed "Progetto 80" – the only attempt at an economic-territorial project elaborated by the National Government in the late 1960s – remained a myth, devoid of any lasting territorial impact.

Throughout this period, Milan played what is generally recognized as a leading role, as the capital of the so called "neo-capitalism", a mode of production characterized by the dominant presence of the big industrial companies but also by socio-spatial forms of regulation centred on capital/labour relationships. In this sense, the "Fordist industrial city" does not exclusively concern the economic reality, simultaneously regarding the various aspects of constantly changing societal territorial organization. Such a steady, territorial "assembly" was a result of specific social and spatial conflicts which concurred to shape the metropolitan context. During those years, the major role of the regional capital of Lombardy is seen as separate from and in contrast to the rest of the metropolitan area. The strength of Milan could count on a larger hinterland capable of absorbing the spatial contradictions of the impetuous growth of that period: for example, the many "dormitory" neighbourhoods or the localization of "intrusive" infrastructures (prisons, incinerators, and so on) that find space outside the city. These are the costs of a massive spatial concentration which characterized the main urban reality of the country and its centre/periphery relationships at various scales.

Territorial deconcentration, or lost spatial hierarchy

The failed goals of various public programs and plans – the territorial rebalancing of the development by means of public investment – surprisingly seemed to be achieved by an impressive and unplanned process of territorial deconcentration by firms and populations. This is a general trend, which involves all the late industrialized Western societies. With different rhythms and intensity, this process also concerns Italy from the 1970s and over the following decades, having a strong impact on regional patterns of development.

In this period, the simultaneous urban decline of the larger industrial cities and the emergence of peripheral and diffused local systems connected to medium and small industrial firms (such as the *industrial districts*: Pyke, Becattini and Sengenberger, 1990; or *areas of specialized production*: Garofoli, 2003),[7] extended the range of territorial situations and diversified the same "paths of development". This is the same theme of the so called *Third Italy* (Bagnasco, 1977)[8] or Nec-model (North East Central-model: Fuà, 1983), surpassing the "dual vision" of Italy historical development and the North/ South divide. The territorial diffusion of the development in this phase relied on the widespread presence of favourable conditions such as welfare infrastructures – public services outcome of layered investment over time – and a few non-intentional effects. For example, in the case of transport policy which having focused on road mobility, shifted towards more flexible localization factors, supporting the diffuse industrialization processes (the geographical distribution of the *Made in Italy* productions confirms this territorial pattern).

If these processes reflect regional and macro-regional trajectories, returning back to observe the "centre", the main industrial cities suffered the backlash and entered a period of profound crisis. The impact of this crisis was quite clearly identifiable in the loss of the share of employment, the decline in the urban population, and an overall weakening of the socio-economic urban structure. As always, the causes are rather diversified; but, mostly, they concern the crisis of the same foundations of the Fordist's accumulation: the sunset of the standardized mass production and the appearance of an alternative social demand for customized goods (Piore and Sabel, 1984).[9] Furthermore, the crisis of the major manufacturing plants in the urban centre corresponded with high levels of social conflict, rising costs in the central localization for firms and families, and the deterioration in the quality of urban life (also due to the increasing urban congestion and strong environmental diseconomies), creating a real risk of urban paralysis and a collapse in the social reproduction of the city.

In this difficult context, Milan is no exception, but it has been able to endure the crisis without disastrous consequences. Thanks to its multisectorial economic base and its spatial flexibility pivoted on its wider metropolitan context, the spontaneous "tertiary transition" of the city during the

1980s allowed the city to transform an important part of its economy into a mature industrial and creative city.

As regards the urban changes, this is the phase of the great "industrial dismantlement" of the metropolitan core, with the abandonment of many factories, often in places becoming quasi-central, and with the emerging theme of the urban renewal and regeneration of the marginal fabric across the whole city (Figure 1.6). Simply in the municipality of Milan, more than 5 million sqm are involved in this spatial restructuring process, although the timing of the actual transformations will expand in the following decades involving other former industrial situations in the enlarged urban region, such as Sesto San Giovanni or Rho, just to name a few.[10]

The complexity of these spatial transformations affects the growing fragmentation of the decision-making network, that are metropolitan no less than that of the city (Gualini, 2005; Gonzàlez, 2009), and this aspect contributes to creating difficulties in the converging various interests on several occasions of development. This is without considering the huge problems of clientelism and corruption, which were subsequently discovered when Milan became known as the "tangentopoli" (or "kickbackcity": Gonzàlez, 2009) in the early 1990s.

A peculiar spatial conjuncture: Milan in the "great contraction"

The recent phase characterized by a continuing worldwide economic recession (interpreted by some in terms of a *great contraction*) is combined with the steady diffusion of a shrinking city dynamic. Clearly, this phenomenon takes on specific forms in different regional contexts. As regards the Milanese spatial reality, we need to consider the unusual combination between two different dimensions. First, an evident *metropolitan recentralization* of which the metropolitan "core" is the driver witnessed in the profound transformation of numerous construction sites over the last fifteen years, and second, the consolidation of the "jump of scale" in urban geography, with the perpetuation of a type of *urban regionalization* process already ongoing for at least thirty years.

This double perspective also covers recent socio-economic data: after a long period, the Milan municipal area starts to increase in terms of population (between 2011–2014, it grew from approximately 1,242,000 to 1,337,000 inhabitants)[11] and levels of employment (the loss of manufacturing jobs in the city is less than in other metropolitan contexts and in the rise of private services occupation figures). At the same time, the socio-demographical dynamics show the consolidation of some historical spatial trajectories (Figure 1.5) – such as the area of Brianza and the transverse

Piedmont corridor, above all in the segment towards Bergamo – and the emergence of East and South-East contexts in the direction of Lodi and Pavia (Centro studi PIM, 2016).

The permanence of these seemingly contradictory trends points to a certain, problematic, distance from most influential interpretations such as "regional urbanization" as a part of a general "post-metropolitan" process (Soja, 2011, 2013). The particular Milanese dynamism, in line with continental specificity (Le Gales and Bagnasco, 2000), seems to require a more careful capability to interpret the socio-economic contextual dimensions, and the combination between various situations: those most dynamic being both inside and outside the city of Milan, as a part of a broader trend of "poor metropolization" with the widespread presence of the working poor characterizing the inequalities of an enlarged context (Centro studi PIM, 2016). Only this attention to "local" specificities of urbanization processes can bring an original contribution to the general reflection on the forms of "extended urbanization" which characterized the current planetary spatial conditions (Brenner, 2014; Brenner and Schmid, 2014).

Conclusion

For the reasons explained above, in the case of Milan, we can talk about an "urban regionalization" tendency, which has to be considered with two distinct meanings: first of all, an enlarged urbanization process that is not generated by a single metropolitan nucleus but by an urban/territorial constellation of centres (often of medium size), in line with "global city-region" or "mega-city region" interpretations (Scott, 2001; Hall and Pain, 2006). The second notion of "urban regionalization" reflects its geographical meaning and relates to the same term, *regionalization*, by which a specific context is subjected to a continuous process of differentiation and internal articulation affecting its spatial division of labour. From an economic perspective, more than a banal post-industrial image (the common ideology trumpeted since the 1980s), Milan's urban region has shifted towards a combination of conception-oriented activities[12] and "industrial" production (Figure 1.4). The same term "industrial" seems to characterize various sectors and clusters, such as some historical industrial districts in evolution (furniture, metal engineering, precision mechanics) and includes new fields of activity, for instance the biotechnology cluster, and traditional service activity such as business tourism, which evolves into an "industrial" organization with new and mutual interdependence.

In this general framework, Milan and its ruling classes have operated for a long time, favouring the spontaneous growth and "natural" disposition of the city regarding economic and social development. The continuing absence of an intentional, strategic, positioning of the city is the other face of this favourable inclination towards spontaneous development and implicit trust in the "creative" strength of the market. Only the recent economic crisis and the new opportunities highlighted by the success of the Expo 2015 (Bolocan Goldstein, 2015) seem to have created new conditions for a strategic proposition and public targets for Milan. From this perspective, a more active promotion of Milan globally in the choice of the new Metropolitan Mayor, Giuseppe Sala,[13] could attract more foreign investment and also host important international agencies (such as the EMA – European Medicine Agency).[14] If this networking capability is able to merge with a new approach to the spatial and functional implementation of some of the main territorial projects – e.g., the "Science and technology park" in the post-Expo site in between Milan and Rho,[15] or the "City of health and research" in the previous Falck sites in Sesto San Giovanni[16] – the positioning of Milan could be advantageous in bringing a more aware vision of its own spatial development possibilities.

Notes

1   Following Jane Jacobs's ideas, Peter Taylor argues that the "inherent complexity of cities distinguishes them from all other settlements – adding – *every* city is extraordinary (they) are astonishing in their economic growth potential and cultural vitality, and amazing in their societal resilience" (Taylor, 2013, p. 3).

2   As anticipated in Chapter 1, the geographical profile of the *Milan Metropolitan Region*, defined by OECD's *Territorial review*, includes the current provincial areas of Varese, Como, Lecco, Monza and Brianza, Como, Bergamo, Lodi, Pavia and Novara (OECD, 2006). A similar geographical dimension has focused on the territorial strategic project "City of cities", promoted by the Province of Milan (Balducci, Fedeli and Pasqui, 2011).

3   The sociologist Aldo Bonomi talks about a "jump of scale" of the former "industrial triangle" (Turin-Milan-Genoa) in an enlarged one: Turin-Ancona-Trieste, with Milan in the middle, in a strategic position (Bonomi, 2013).

4   The so-called diffused territorial suburb of Milan. The "Comune of Corpi Santi" (Holy Bodies) was established in the period under Austrian domination, and realized in 1782. It was annexed to Milan in 1873.

5   It is in the second half of the Eighteenth Century which emerged the "long epoch" of the industrial era – interpreted by the Harvard historian Charles S. Mayer. In tension with Hobsbawm's approach (Hobsbawm, 1994), concerning the "Short Twentieth Century 1914–1991", Mayer privileges a unitary vision of the modern industrial society focusing his attention on three interdependent features of social development: spatial organization (the principle of territoriality and the spatial domination within national-state borders), the technological foundations of economic development and the changing nature of the social structure (Mayer, 1997).

6   In particular, the Inter-municipality plan's debate, at the beginning of 1960s, was an important example of a politicization of the metropolitan arena, with the

left-wing culture and parties favoured of decentralization of the main functions in a wider metropolitan territory and the Christian Democrats exponents who were in favour of an alternative territorial pattern (the so-called Linear development hypothesis, a territorial corridor along the foothill Northern axis) (Bolocan Goldstein, 2005).

7 Sebastiano Brusco states that "an industrial district is a set of companies located in a relatively small geographical area; that the said companies work, either directly or indirectly, for the same end market; that their shared range of values and body of knowledge is so important that they define a cultural environmental; and that they are linked to one another by very specific relations in a complex mix of competition and co-operation" (Brusco, 1992, p. 177).

8 According to this definition (Bagnasco, 1977), the Third Italy was composed of Friuli Venezia Giulia, Trentino Alto Adige, Veneto, Emilia Romagna, Tuscany, Umbria and Marche. The North-West regions were Lombardy, Piedmont, Valle d'Aosta and Liguria; those remaining were part were part of the South Italy.

9 In their influential work they talked about "flexible specialization" process (Piore and Sabel, 1984), that invested both the large firms organization and the local systems based on medium-small firms and that will move towards the "re-emergence of regional economies" (Sabel, 1994).

10 See Chapters 7 and 8.

11 The growth is undoubtedly driven by foreign component: in the period between 2005–2015, in the Municipal area it raised from 10 per cent to 18.4 per cent, while in the Metropolitan City it raised from 6.8 per cent to 13.7 per cent (Centro studi PIM, 2016). In the same period, in Milan Municipality, the proportion of young people (under 25), increased from 18.8 per cent to 22.3 per cent, while those over 65 decreased from 25.2 per cent to 23.5 per cent (Centro studi PIM, 2016).

12 Activities in horizontal services that "aim at devising the conceptual blueprint of products and often intervene at the top of various sectorial supply chains, such as industrial design" (OECD, 2006, p. 45).

13 See Chapter 10.

14 Brexit has opened a new scenario for Milan with the opportunity to reinforce its European and global profile.

15 See Chapter 8.

16 See Chapter 7.

References

Bagnasco, A. (1977). *Tre Italie: La problematica territoriale dello sviluppo italiano.* Bologna: Il Mulino.

Balducci, A., Fedeli, V. and Pasqui, G. (2011). *Strategic planning for contemporary urban regions: City of cities: A project.* London: Routledge.

Becattini, G. (1990). The Marshallian industrial district as a socio-economic notion. In: F. Pyke, G. Becattini and W. Sengenberger, eds., *Industrial district and inter-firm co-operation in Italy.* Geneva: International Institute for Labor Studies, pp. 37–51.

Bolocan Goldstein, M. (2005). Confini mobili: Sviluppo urbano e rapporti territoriali nel Milanese. In: M. Bolocan Goldstein and B. Bonfantini, eds., *Milano incompiuta: Interpretazioni urbanistiche del mutamento.* Milano: Franco Angeli, pp. 169–184.

46   *Matteo Bolocan Goldstein*

Bolocan Goldstein, M. (2015). Post-expo geographical scenarios. *Urbanistica*, 155, pp. 118–122.

Bolocan Goldstein, M. and Puttili, M. (2011). Geografie del Nord Territori e funzioni nella mondializzazione. *Atti e rassegna tecnica*, 144, pp. 3–4.

Bonomi, A. (2013). *Il capitalismo in-finito: Indagine sui territori della crisi.* Torino: Einaudi.

Brenner, N. ed. (2014). *Implosions/explosions: Towards a study of planetary urbanization.* Berlin: Jovis Verlag.

Brenner, N. and Schmid, C. (2014). The 'Urban Age' in question. *International Journal of Urban and Regional Research*, 38(3), pp. 731–755.

Brusco, S. (1992). Small firms and the provision of real services. In: F. Pyke and W. Sengenberger, eds., *Industrial districts and local economic regeneration.* Geneva: International Institute for Labor Studies, pp. 177–196.

Centro Studi PIM. (2016). Spazialità metropolitane: Economia, società e territorio. *Argomenti & Contributi*, 15, Special Issue.

Fuà, G. (1983). L'industrializzazione del Nord Est e del Centro. In: G. Fuà G. and C. Zacchia, eds., *Industrializzazione senza fratture.* Bologna: Il Mulino, pp. 7–45.

Garofoli, G. (2003). Distretti industriali e processo di globalizzazione: trasformazioni e nuove traiettorie. In: G. Garofoli, ed., *Impresa e territorio.* Bologna: Il Mulino, pp. 539–571.

González, S. (2009). (Dis)connecting Milan(ese): Deterritorialised urbanism and disempowering politics in globalising cities. *Environment and Planning A*, pp. 31–47.

Gramsci, A. (1975), *Quaderni del carcere*, edizione critica dell'Istituto Gramsci, V. Gerratana, ed., Torino: Einaudi.

Gualini, E. (2005). The Milan urban region and local cooperation: Framing local governance by innovating policies. In: F. Hendriks, P. Tops and V. van Stipdonk, eds., *Urban-regional governance in the European union: Practices and prospects.* The Hague: Elsevier, pp. 143–171.

Hall, P. and Pain, K. eds. (2006). *The polycentric metropolis: Learning from megacity regions in Europe.* London: Earthscan.

Hobsbawm, E.J. (1994). *Age of extremes: The short twentieth century 1914–1991.* Random House: Pantheon Books.

Le Gales, P. and Bagnasco, A. eds. (2000). *Cities in contemporary Europe.* Cambridge: Cambridge University Press.

Mayer, C.S. (1997). Secolo corto o epoca lunga? L'unità storica dell'età industriale e le trasformazioni della territorialità. In: C. Pavone, ed., *Novecento. I tempi della storia.* Roma: Donzelli, pp. 45–77.

OECD. (2006). *Territorial reviews: Milan, Italy.* Paris: OECD Publishing.

Piore, M.J. and Sabel C.F. (1984). *The second industrial divide: Possibilities for prosperity.* New York: Basic Books.

Sabel, C.F. (1989). Flexible specialization and the re-emergence of regional economies. In: A. Amin, ed., *Post-fordism. A reader.* Oxford: Basil Blackwell, pp. 101–156.

Scott, A.J. ed. (2001). *Global city-regions: Trends, theory, policy.* Oxford: Oxford University Press.

Soja, E.W. (2011). Regional urbanization and the end of metropolis era. In: G. Bridge and S. Watson, eds., *The new Blackwell companion to the city*. Hoboken, NJ: Wiley-Blackwell, pp. 679–689.

Soja, E.W. (2013). Regional urbanization and third wave cities. *City: Analysis of Urban Trends, Culture, Theory, Policy, Action,* 17(5), pp. 688–694.

Taylor, P.J. (2004). *World city network: A global urban analysis.* London, New York: Routledge.

Taylor, P.J. (2013). *Extraordinary cities: Millennia of moral syndromes, world-system and city/state relations.* Cheltenham, UK, Northampton, US: Edward Elgar.

3 The attractiveness of Milan and the spatial patterns of international firms

Ilaria Mariotti

Introduction

Over the last three decades, the proportion of people living in urban areas has increased throughout the global economy. The number of cities in the world with a population of more than one million grew from 115 in 1960 to 416 in 2000; those with more than 4 million increased from 18 to 53, and those with more than 12 million jumped from one to 11 (Venables, 2006). By 2006, more people lived in urban areas than in non-urban areas worldwide for the first time in history (Mastercard, 2008). Moreover, large cities are predicted to contribute 61 per cent of the world's GDP by 2030, and 40 per cent of the 50 largest cities in the world in terms of constant-prices GDP will be Chinese (Ernest and Young, 2015). This trend suggests that it is becoming increasingly important for people employed in high-knowledge and high-skills activities to be geographically close (Moretti, 2012; Iammarino and McCann, 2013). Tacit knowledge still requires close contact to be exchanged and shared, facilitated by co-location, and even through regular or less regular travel (McCann, 2008). The key role played by cities is nothing new. Jane Jacobs (1970) stressed that cities are the engine of national, regional, and global economic growth because they offer advantages related to agglomeration (Glaeser, 2011) and connectedness with the rest of the world. Agglomeration economies, and specifically urbanization economies, enhance creativity (Florida, 2005), efficiency (Combes et al., 2012), and innovation (Acs, 2002); moreover, the great connectedness of global cities make geographical distance less of an obstacle for firms (Friedman, 1986; Sassen, 1991, 2012; Castells, 1996).

On one side, global cities are attractive for foreign multinational enterprises (henceforth MNEs) because of their ability to reduce the liability of foreignness (Nachum, 2003; Goerzen et al., 2014); on the other, countries are increasingly competing to attract inward foreign direct investments (hereinafter, FDIs) because of the potential benefits (Lipsey, 2002;

Crescenzi, Gagliardi and Iammarino, 2015). As extensively emphasized in the literature, MNEs are more likely to adopt new technologies, achieve higher productivity, and therefore employ a more highly-skilled labour force. Therefore, the affiliates of foreign MNEs – that is inward FDIs – generate technological and managerial cumulative effects on the local environment in which they settle, and the spillovers spurring from the interaction between foreign multinational enterprises and the local context. MNEs may improve the innovative capabilities, productivity, and competitiveness of local firms. However, MNEs may also have a negative effect on the local area by monopolizing the market, and displacing the domestic production of inputs.

This chapter focuses on the attractiveness behaviour of the Lombardy NUTS2 region and of the metropolitan city of Milan[1] towards inward FDIs, stressing the privileged role played by the "city" as the location for MNEs. The focus on Milan is due to its significant attractiveness within the Italian context: by 2015 it registered about 34 per cent of inward FDIs, employing 30.4 per cent of workers and producing about 34 per cent of turnover. Besides, the Italian MNEs located in Milan undertook about 16 per cent of the Italian outward FDIs, employing 17.8 per cent of workers abroad and registering 12.3 per cent of the turnover. Besides, the analysis of the geography of firm location shows that the headquarters of foreign affiliates in knowledge intensive services privilege the Milan central area, and recently few global players in ICT sector settled in the new development area of Porta Nuova-Garibaldi. Different location patterns characterize FDIs' in wholesale and retail trade and transport and logistics. Specifically, logistics sprawl outside – but near to – the city to overcome excessive agglomeration and congestions problems.

Firm location factors and the renewed role of the city

Factors determining the location of firms have been studied by the following four main branches of the location theory (for a review see McCann, 2002; Brouwer, Mariotti and van Ommeren, 2004; Arauzo, 2005): neoclassical, behavioural, institutional, and evolutionary. The literature on FDI determinants indicates that MNEs allocate their investments among countries to maximize their risk-adjusted profits (Caves, 1974), which may depend on three groups of factors that are well summarized in the eclectic OLI paradigm developed by Dunning (1979, 2009). They are: (i) "Ownership advantages", that is, firm-specific factors enabling the firm to grow more successfully than competitors in home or host countries (i.e., proprietary technology and management expertise); (ii) "Location advantages", that is, location-specific factors in the host country that make it the best location for the firm to do business (i.e., cheap labour costs, growing market, and good infrastructure); and (iii) "Internalization advantages", that is, factors associated with the firm's trade-off between FDI and exporting or licensing (i.e., trade barriers and difficulties in finding a trustworthy licensee).

Both location theory and research on "L" advantages have identified the following main location determinants for manufacturing firms: (i) "traditional location factors" (land, labour, market, agglomeration economies, transportation costs); (ii) infrastructures, services and intangible assets; (iii) environmental and social context; (iv) policy framework; (v) information costs. However, theoretical and empirical studies affirm that the same factors may be relevant for the service sector (for a review see Mariotti, 2015).

Studies on the location of MNEs have always focused on investing countries, while, more recently, specific attention has been placed on the location choices at sub-national level (for a review see Castellani and Santangelo, 2016): NUTS2 region (Castellani and Pieri, 2016; Basile, Castellani, Crescenzi and Iammarino, 2015), and city level (Goerzen et al., 2014; Castellani and Santangelo, 2016). Castellani and Pieri (2016) find that 10 per cent of the most attractive European NUTS2 regions make 26 times more FDIs than the 10 per cent of the NUTS2 regions on the lower part of the scale. Besides, Basile, Castellani, and Crescenzi (2015) state that the standard deviation of investments projects financed by European NUTS2 regions is 1.8 times bigger than the average, reaching 2.5 and 2.2 for French and Italian regions. Goerzen et al. (2014) and Castellani and Santangelo (2016) focus on the attractiveness of the city, and specifically global cities, which offer firms advantages linked to urbanization and localization economies, which enhance creativity (Florida, 2005) – they are the favourable location for talents and the best creative minds – efficiency (Combes et al., 2012), and innovation (Acs, 2002); market size and potential; skilled labour force availability and business opportunities; transportation accessibility; connectedness[2] with the rest of the world. Specifically, Castellani and Santangelo (2016) in the analysis based on 111,310 greenfield FDIs, undertaken within global cities[3] in 2003–2015, find that 57 per cent of coordination activities (headquarters) are located in global cities, and in their metropolitan areas, which are sufficiently proximate and well-connected to global cities to enjoy the liability of foreignness' reduction and lower congestion costs and tax payments. On the other hand, R&D related activities are more likely to be located in moderately global cities, which offer urban contexts that are especially conducive to innovation (Feldman and Audretsch, 1999), while peripheral cities primarily attract cross-border production activities. Specifically, there is a higher concentration of investments in South East Asia than in North America, mainly because there are fewer cities in emerging economies. Europe is the area with the largest number of cities that attract at least one investment, and inward FDIs in Italy are mainly concentrated in two top level global cities: Milan and Rome.

Nevertheless, even negative aspects characterize global cities, i.e., excessive agglomeration and congestions problems that lead to higher costs and lower quality of life. This explains why some MNEs' activities (i.e., logistics) that require large areas in which to operate are mainly located outside – but near to – global cities (Holl and Mariotti, 2017). The same holds true for R&D activities that require the construction of large laboratories, which is best done outside global cities, in areas that are still agglomerated and which offer a quality of life that is attractive to the most skilled (Castellani, 2016). Finally, peripheral areas should attract more labour intensive activities, in which production costs are relatively higher.

Milan attractiveness[4]

Italy is considered a multinational follower due to its attractiveness towards inward FDIs, and internationalization propensity fostering outward FDIs, which is below the European average (Mariotti and Mutinelli, 2016). According to UNCTAD (2015), in 2014 the ratio between inward FDI stock and GDP was 17.4 per cent in Italy, and 49.6 per cent in the EU27, with the UK showing 56.5 per cent, Spain 51.3 per cent, France 25.6 per cent, and Germany 19.3 per cent. This low attractiveness is even confirmed by the World Economic Forum (2016), which ranks Italy 43rd, after all other industrialized countries. As concerns the Italian internationalization propensity, in 2014 the ratio between outward FDI stock and GDP was 25.5 per cent in Italy, and 56.4 per cent in the EU27, with the UK showing 53.8 per cent, France 44.9 per cent, Spain 47.3 per cent, and Germany 47 per cent (UNCTAD, 2015). According to Basile, Benfratello, and Castellani (2005), the Italian regions attract significantly less than their observable characteristics, with the exception of Lombardy. Among the main obstacles to firm location there are bureaucratic efficiency and the ability of the legal system to enforce property rights; besides, tax competition does not appear to be a very effective policy measure in the presence of significant agglomeration forces.

The most recent data show that the internationalization of the Lombardy region, and of Milan, is significant within the Italian context, even though Lombardy is home to just 16.5 per cent of inhabitants, 17.9 per cent of working local units and 22.3 per cent of employees (Mutinelli, 2016). The main location factors attracting MNEs to the metropolitan city of Milan are strategic geographic position, good accessibility, high skilled labour force availability, market size and market demand, urbanization, and localization economies. In 2015, Lombardy registered 26.9 per cent and 31.3 per cent respectively of the country's overall exports and imports; the Italian MNEs located in Lombardy have undertaken 34 per cent of outward FDI, employ 36.2 per cent of the total workers abroad, and account for 23.5 per cent of turnover. The region attracted 49.2 per cent of the inward FDI, 44 per cent of local employment, and 44.4 per cent of turnover (Mutinelli, 2016). As for the Metropolitan City of Milan, it hosted Italian MNEs that undertook about 16 per cent of the Italian outward FDIs, employed 17.8 per cent of the workers abroad, and registered 12.3 per cent of turnover. Besides, Milan attracted about 34 per cent of inward FDIs, employing 30.4 per cent of workers and producing about 34 per cent of the turnover (Table 3.1).[5]

The Italian MNEs located in Lombardy and Milan mainly invested in Western Europe, in Latin America, and in the Middle East, while inward investments to Milan and Lombardy tend to come from the same countries of origin as those throughout the rest of the country: Western Europe, North America, and Japan. Nevertheless, the importance of North American, Asian and Pacific investment areas is, on average, more significant in Milan than in the rest of the country. Specifically, in 2008–2015 the number of Milanese firms participated in by Chinese MNEs has more than tripled, passing from 20 to 69 units, while the number of employees increased six-fold (Mutinelli, 2016). Two significant examples are the 40 per cent shareholding of Shanghai Electric in Ansaldo Energia in 2014, and the acquisition of Pirelli by ChemChina in 2015. The attractiveness of Milan towards the more remote countries, with a strong cultural distance (Hofstede, 1980), like China, confirms its role as a global city reducing the liability of foreignness for foreign investors.

As concerns the sectors, the Italian MNEs are specialized in medium-high and high technological intensity sectors (pharmaceutical, chemical, mechanics, electric, electronic, and optics), rubber and plastic products, and in the publishing industry, while foreign MNEs invested in almost all the sectors, thus confirming the strong multi-sectorial composition of the

Table 3.1 Inward and outward FDIs in Lombardy region and Milan province at January 1st 2015

	Milan province		Lombardy	
	N.	*Share on Italy (%)*	*N.*	*Share on Italy (%)*
Outward FDIs				
Outward FDIs (n.)	4,826	15.9	10,261	34.0
- Employees (n.)	272,645	17.8	556,079	36.2
- Turnover (billion euro)	68,882	12.3	132,044	23.5
Inward FDIs				
Inward FDIs (n.)	3,029	33.9	4,395	49.2
- Employees (n.)	288,552	30.4	417,092	44.0
- Turnover (billion euro)	168,908	33.9	220,787	44.4

Source: Mutinelli (2016, p. 87)

Table 3.2 Inward FDIs in Lombardy region and Milan province by sectors at
January 1st 2015

	Inward FDIs			Employees of inward FDIs		
	Absolute values		Share Milan/Italy (%)	Absolute values		Share on Italy (%)
	Milan	Lombardy		Milan	Lombardy	
Mining industry	5	8	16.1	108	311	5.3
Manufacturing industry*	536	1,136	17.5	94,102	183,106	18.8
Energy, gas, water	64	89	25.9	5,265	5,668	40.3
Construction	46	66	20.3	3,634	4,218	31.6
Wholesale	1,270	1,785	41.3	58,181	72,310	48.7
Transport and logistics	138	196	27.6	19,393	24,284	34.7
ICT services	290	325	51.6	50,230	53,070	37.3
Other services	689	808	48.1	58,525	75,422	52.6
Total	3,029	4,395	33.9	288,552	417,092	30.4

Note: * it includes "other manufacturing industries"
Source: author's elaboration on Mutinelli (2016)

regional and metropolitan city's economy (Table 3.2). Milan and Lombardy have always been considered the best location for MNEs wishing to invest in Italy to gain new markets. These areas are attractive for manufacturing and services, although both the tertiarization process of the regional economy, and the progressive reduction of the manufacturing industry weight, took place. Albeit the descending trend, the presence of foreign manufacturing MNEs in the metropolitan city of Milan is not negligible, mainly as concerns the higher technological intensity, and the medium-low technological sectors (food and editorial) both in absolute terms and with reference to the national context. As far as the service sector is concerned, the metropolitan city hosts a concentration of foreign affiliates operating in wholesale and retail trade, ICT, and transport and logistics. Specifically, FDIs in wholesale and retail trade choose to be located in Milan because of market proximity and market potential; ICT firms privilege a central location to exploit urbanization economies, while transport and logistics firms tend to sprawl in suburban locations and with good accessibility likely due to their lower factor prices and land availability (Bowen, 2008; Holl, Mariotti, 2017).

Among the first forty foreign MNEs[6] investing in Italy (see Mutinelli, 2016) 17 settled their head office in Lombardy, and among those, 11 in the Metropolitan city of Milan (Table 3.3). Milan attracted ICT investments with Accenture in the top position – employing more than 10,000 workers in its Italian affiliates – followed by Hewlett Packard and NTT with retail and

Table 3.3 Global players located in Lombardy and their ranking at December 31st 2014

Foreign Group	Ranking	Country	NUTS3 Province of Location	Activity
DUSSMANN	1	DE	Bergamo	Other professional services
ACCENTURE, INC.	2	US	Milan	ICT
WHIRLPOOL CORP.	4	US	Varese	Electrical appliances
ABB ASEA BROWN BOVERI	9	CH	Milan	Electro-mechanics
TECHINT S.A.	10	AR	Bergamo	Iron and steel industry, engineering
NESTLE' S.A.	15	CH	Milan	Food and beverage
HEWLETT-PACKARD CO.	18	US	Milan	ICT, consultancy
LVMH MOET HENNESSY – LOUIS VUITTON S.A.	20	FR	Milan	Retail trade
NOVARTIS AG	21	CH	Varese	Pharmaceutical
METRO AG	23	DE	Bergamo	Wholesale trade
DEUTSCHE POST AG	24	DE	Milan	Transport and logistics
ELECTRICITE' DE FRANCE S.A. – EDF	26	FR	Milan	Electric energy and gas
VEOLIA ENVIRONNEMENT S.A.	28	FR	Milan	Water, facility management
DEUTSCHE BAHN AG	32	DE	Milan	Transport and logistics
SIEMENS AG	33	DE	Milan	Electro-mechanics, healthcare
NTT – NIPPON TELEGRAPH AND TELEPHONE CORP.	37	JP	Milan	ICT
SCHNEIDER ELECTRIC S.A.	39	FR	Bergamo	Electro-mechanics

Source: author's elaboration on Mutinelli (2016) and Reprint database.

wholesale trade and transport and logistics following. As stated above, the foreign affiliates in wholesale and retail trade settled in Milan because of market proximity and market potential. Similarly, the investments undertaken by the logistics players Deutsche Post and Deutsche Bahn are driven by strong urbanization and agglomeration economies, and good accessibility (Mariotti, Maltese and Boscacci, 2012; Brouwer and Mariotti, 2014; Mariotti, 2015).

The other foreign affiliates are specialized in manufacturing (electro-mechanics, iron and steel industry, food and beverage, and pharmaceutical), electric energy-gas, and water-facility management. These investments tend to settle within the existing industrial agglomerations to gain from localization economies and to reduce the liability of foreignness. Specifically, mechanical firms are clustered in Lecco, Varese, Como, and Bergamo, which also hosts firms specialized in rubber and plastic, home furniture in Monza and Brianza, and chemical and pharmaceutical industry in East Milan. Besides, South-East Milan, where Linate airport is located, and Malpensa airport area accommodate logistics firms (Figure 1.4) (Goldstein, 2016).

An interesting trend concerns the location of the head offices of foreign ICT multinationals in the new urban transformation area of the city. As an example, Google, Samsung, and Microsoft settled in the Porta Nuova area (Figure 1.6), which has been recently regenerated, and where new skyscrapers have been built (i.e. Unicredit bank head office, and the residential building "Vertical Forest").[7]

Conclusion

This chapter aimed to explore the attractiveness of Lombardy and Milan in terms of inward and outward FDIs, focusing on the location determinants. The analysis confirmed the poor attractiveness of Italy, as a whole, and consequently the low embeddedness towards high tech foreign MNEs, which has led to the closure of important foreign R&D centres. By contrast, it has highlighted the key role of Lombardy and of Milan as a global city that represents a privileged location for domestic and foreign MNEs. Recent studies emphasized the key role of cities in attracting investments, and specifically that advanced services investments tend to be located in main global cities, while innovative projects are more willing to be concentrated in a few centres of excellence (Acs, 2002). R&D and innovative projects require an agglomeration of talent without excessive congestion costs, easy proximity to universities, limited land, and premises costs.

As extensively described within the theoretical and empirical literature on the effects of MNEs on the host country (see Lipsey, 2002), attracting MNEs becomes crucial for a country since firms operating in international markets are more likely to adopt new technologies, achieve higher productivity, and therefore employ a more highly skilled labour force. Working on the global scale, requires significant investments in innovation in order to stay competitive. In advanced economies, this last aspect plays a crucial role in enhancing local and regional innovation capabilities. There is a strong relationship between firms' and workers' competitiveness, and workers' competitiveness crucially depends on skills (education and training) (Barzotto et al., 2016). Besides, scholars have highlighted both the direct and indirect effects of MNEs on (a) performance; (b) employment and skills; (c) trade; and (d) balance of payments in the host country. Direct effects are typical of the micro-level studies and investigate output and employment, while indirect effects concern the company's supply chain and the broader business environment in which it operates (Mariotti and Piscitello, 2007; Castellani, Mariotti and Piscitello, 2008; Elia, Mariotti and Piscitello, 2009).

Recently, few studies have been carried out on the relationship between FDIs and the performance of Lombardy (Altomonte, Saggiorato and Sforza, 2012; Altomonte, 2014). Altomonte, Saggiorato and Sforza (2012) in the comparative analysis about inward FDIs performance in Lombardy and in other EU NUTS2 regions find that the presence of inward FDIs, downstream domestic firms in Lombardy, had a positive impact on the local firms due to a "learning by supplying" effect. Specifically, domestic suppliers gained from their foreign customers in terms of productive efficiency, technology and brand. The study by Altomonte (2014) on the effects of inward FDIs on Lombardy shows that the presence of multinational groups represents an opportunity for local firms to enter global networks. It has been demonstrated that a higher presence of inward FDIs belonging to foreign multinational groups generates a larger flow of added value both produced and received by domestic firms, and therefore, greater participation in the global value chains.

The analysis of the attractiveness of Lombardy and Milan and the studies on the effects of inward FDIs on the host areas suggest that specific policies might be advocated, such as a policy tailored on the country's supply of resources and competences, focusing on three pillars: (i) talents and expertise; (ii) advanced manufacturing; (iii) the city (Mariotti and Piscitello, 2012). In the past more than today, Italy used to offer an excellent educational system able to promote the scientific and technic culture. The country, therefore, needs to reinforce this system and to be able to train expertise of the industrial system, and should be willing to foster the international circulation of brains, mainly on graduate and post graduate levels. Since Italy is the EU's second manufacturing country, the second pillar focuses on the promotion of advanced manufacturing, even bringing it back from abroad through re-shoring and back-shoring initiatives. Finally, the role of the city's quality in attracting investments is highly significant. As previously stated, the attractiveness of a city is due not only to its urban agglomeration economies but also to the interconnectedness and the concentration of the economic and political powers (Rodriguez-Pose and Zademach, 2006).

Acknowledgments

I gratefully acknowledge the support of Marco Mutinelli in providing data on inward FDI in Lombardy, besides, I thank the editors of the book for their useful suggestions. The usual disclaimer applies.

Notes

1 The Metropolitan City of Milan (Italian: Città Metropolitana di Milano) is a metropolitan city in the Lombardy region; its capital is the city of Milan. Since the year 2015 it replaced the NUTS3 province of Milan, and includes the city of Milan and other 133 municipalities or municipalities.
2 The high degree of interconnectedness characterizing global cities reduces search and information costs regarding the environment; besides, it creates a favourable environment for FDIs and facilitates the transfer of tangible and intangible goods (Castellani and Santangelo, 2016).
3 The Global cities, which have been considered, belong to the Globalization and World Cities (Gawc) classification (see: www.lboro.ac.uk/gawc).
4 This section presents the data on inward and outward FDIs in Italy provided by the Reprint database, developed by the Politecnico di Milano, and sponsored by ICE. For a recent review of inward and outward FDIs in the Lombardy region and Milan, see Mutinelli (2016).
5 A significant share of outward FDIs is registered in the cities of Turin and Rome because they host the headquarters of some large, international Italian industrial groups: FIAT, ENEL, ENI, and Finmeccanica.
6 The first forty global players investing in Italy have been selected based on the number of workers employed in their affiliates (Mutinelli, 2016).
7 The Vertical Forest (Bosco Verticale), designed by Boeri Studio, was inaugurated in October 2014 in Milan in the Porta Nuova Isola area, as part of a wider renovation project.

References

Acs, Z. (2002). *Innovation and the growth of cities*. Cheltenham: Edward Elgar.
Altomonte, C. (2014). La partecipazione delle imprese lombarde alle global value chains. *Milano Produttiva 2013*, Milan Chamber of Commerce Report, 156–173.
Altomonte, C., Saggiorato, L. and Sforza, A. (2012). TNCs' global characteristics and subsidiaries' performance across European regions. *Transnational Corporations*, 21(2), pp. 1–20.
Arauzo, J.M. (2005). Determinant of industrial location: An application for Catalan municipalities. *Papers in Regional Science*, 84(1), pp. 105–120.
Barzotto, M., Corò, G., Mariotti, I. and Mutinelli, M. (2016). Inward FDI and host country labour markets: Evidence from the Italian manufacturing system. *CMET Working Paper*, 3/2016.
Basile, R., Benfratello, L. and Castellani, D. (2005). Attracting foreign direct investments in Europe: Are Italian regions doomed? *Working Paper*, Centro Studi Luca D'Agliano.
Basile, R., Castellani, D., Crescenzi, R., and Iammarino, S. (2015). Quality of governance and inward FDI along the value chain: does within-country heterogeneity

matter? AIB-Mini Conference on Breaking up the global value chain: Possibilities and consequences. Milan, October 29–31.

Bolocan Goldstein, M. (2016). Rapporti territoriali nella grande contrazione: Osservazioni sulla regione metropolitana milanese. *Milano Produttiva 2016*, Milan Chamber of Commerce Report, 131–139.

Bowen, J.T. (2008). Moving places: The geography of warehousing in the US. *Journal of Transport Geography*, 16, pp. 379–387.

Brouwer, A. E. and Mariotti, I. (2014). Firm heterogeneity in multinational and domestic firms in Italian logistics. *European Transport – Trasporti Europei*, 56(8), 1–17.

Brouwer, A.E., Mariotti, I., van Ommeren, J.N. (2004). The firm relocation decision: an empirical investigation. *Annals of Regional Science*, 38: 335–347.

Castellani, D. (2016). La multinazionale va in città. *L'Italia nell'economia internazionale*, ICE Report 2015–2016, Rome, 236–245.

Castellani, D., Mariotti, I. and Piscitello, L. (2008). The impact of outward investments on parent company's employment and skill composition: Evidence from the Italian case. *Structural Change and Economic Dynamics*, 19(1), pp. 81–94.

Castellani, D. and Pieri, F. (2016). Outward investments and productivity: Evidence from European regions. *Regional Studies*, 50(12), pp. 1945–1964.

Castellani, D. and Santangelo, G. (2016). Quo vadis? Cities and the location of cross-border activities. *European International Business Academy Conference*, Vienna.

Castells, M. (1996). *The rise of the network society*. Oxford: Blackwell.

Caves, R.E. (1974). Multinational firms, competition, and productivity in host-country markets. *Economica*, 41, pp. 176–193.

Combes, P.P., Duranton, G., Gobillon, L., Puga, D. and Roux, S. (2012). The productivity advantages of large cities: Distinguishing agglomeration from firm selection. *Econometrica*, 80(6), pp. 2543–2594.

Crescenzi, R., Gagliardi, L. and Iammarino, S. (2015). Foreign multinationals and domestic innovation: Intra-industry effects and firm heterogeneity. *Research Policy*, 44(3), pp. 596–609.

Dunning, J.H. (1979). Explaining changing patterns of international production: In defence of the eclectic theory. *Oxford Bulletin of Economics and Statistics*, 41(4), pp. 269–295.

Dunning, J.H. (2009). Location and the multinational enterprise: John Dunning's thoughts on receiving the Journal of International Business Studies 2008 Decade Award. *Journal of International Business Studies*, 40(1), pp. 20–34.

Elia, S., Mariotti, I. and Piscitello, L. (2009). The impact of outward FDI on the home country's labour demand and skill composition. *International Business Review*, 18, pp 357–372.

Ernst and Young. (2015). *Megatrends 2015: Making sense of a world in motion*. Available at: www.ey.com/Publication/vwLUAssets/ey-megatrends-report-2015/$FILE/ey-megatrends-report-2015.pdf.

Feldman, M.P. and Audretsch, D. (1999). Innovation in cities: Science-based diversity, specialization and localized competition. *European Economic Review*, 43, pp. 409–429.

Florida, R. (2005). *Cities and the creative class*. London: Routledge.

Friedmann, J. (1986). The world city hypothesis. *Development and Change*, 17, pp. 69–83.

Glaeser, E. (2011). *Triumph of the city: How our greatest invention makes us richer, smarter, greener, healthier, and happier.* New York: Penguin.

Goerzen, A., Asmussen, C.G. and Nielsen, B.B. (2014). Global cities and multinational enterprise location strategy. *Journal of International Business Studies,* 44(5), pp. 427–450.

Hofstede, G. (1980). *Culture's consequences: International differences in work-related values.* Beverly Hills, CA: Sage.

Holl, A. and Mariotti, I. (2017). The geography of logistics firm location: The role of accessibility. *Networks and Spatial Economics,* 18, 1–25.

Iammarino, S. and McCann, P. (2013). *Multinationals and economic Geography: Location, technology and innovation.* Cheltenham, UK: Edward Elgar.

Jacobs, J. (1970). *The economy of cities.* New York: Vintage.

Lipsey, R.E. (2002). Home and host country effects of FDI, National Bureau of Economic Research. *NBER Working Papers 9293.*

Mariotti, I. (2015). *Transport and logistics in a globalizing word.* London: Springer.

Mariotti, I., Maltese, I. and Boscacci, F. (2012). Location choice of inward logistics FDI in Italy. In: M. Campagna, A. De Montis, F. Isola, S. Lai, C. Pira and C. Zoppi, eds., *Planning support tools: Policy analysis, implementation and evaluation.* Milan: FrancoAngeli, pp. 1695–1708.

Mariotti, I. and Piscitello, L. (2007). The impact of outward FDI on local employment: Evidence from the Italian case. In: M. Arauzo, D. Liviano and M. Martín, eds., *Entrepreneurship, economic growth and industrial location,* London: Edward Elgar, pp. 299–320.

Mariotti, S. and Mutinelli, M. (2016). *Italia multinazionale 2016: Le partecipazioni italiane all'estero ed estere in Italia.* Soveria Mannelli: Rubbettino Editore.

Mariotti, S. and Piscitello, L. (2012). Linee guida per un'efficace politica di attrazione degli investimenti esteri. *Economia E Politica Industriale,* FrancoAngeli, 1, pp. 139–157.

Mastercard. (2008). *Worldwide centers of commerce index 2008,* Mastercard Insights.

McCann, P. ed. (2002). *Industrial location economics.* Cheltenham, UK: Edward Elgar.

McCann, P. (2008). Globalization and economic geography: The world is curved, not flat. *Cambridge Journal of Regions, Economy and Society,* 1, pp. 351–370.

Moretti, E. (2012). *The new geography of jobs.* New York: Houghton Mifflin Harcourt.

Mutinelli, M. (2016). L'internazionalizzazione tramite investimenti diretti esteri. In: *Camera di Commercio di Milano, Milano Produttiva 2016.* Milano: Camera di Commercio, pp. 83–96.

Nachum, L. (2003). Liability of foreignness in global competition? Financial service affiliates in the city of London. *Strategic Management Journal,* 24(12), 1187–1208.

Rodríguez-Pose, A. and Zademach, H.M. (2006). Industry dynamics in the German merger and acquisitions market. *Tijdschrift Voor Economische En Sociale Geografie,* 97(3), pp. 296–313.

Sassen, S. (1991). *The global city.* Princeton: Princeton University Press.

Sassen, S. (2012). *Cities in a world economy* (4th ed.). Thousand Oaks, CA: Sage.

UNCTAD. (2015). *World investment report,* Geneve.

Venables, A.J. (2006). *Shifts in economic geography and their causes.* Jackson Hole, Wyoming, August 24–26.

4 Creative production and urban regeneration in Milan

Antonella Bruzzese

Introduction

Creative production, as part of the wider field of cultural and creative industry, has become a significant driver in many urban economies, as acknowledged in the international debate about creative cities and work innovation as well as in recent European policies.[1] Besides its role at the economic level, this kind of production, more than others, also has the capacity to influence the reputation and the atmosphere of the neighbourhoods where it is located (Scott, 2000; Storper and Venables, 2004; Neff, 2005) as well as their "attractiveness" (Ingallina, 2010).

The present contribution analyses how, in Milan, the relationship between creative production and urban regeneration has evolved in recent years. The chapter proposes a definition, first, of creative production and then, second, of its spatial localization and concentration in the city, while also considering the role held by a specific temporary and recurrent event in Milan, the *Fuorisalone*. The chapter then explores how these concentrations formed in semi-peripheral areas and finally, proposes some issues for the public agenda.

Creative production

Cultural and creative industries

Some definitions are needed to clarify what creative production is and likewise, what the cultural and creative industry is, since the first one can be considered as a sector of the second. The first definition, provided in 1998 by the British Department of Culture, Media and Sports (DCMS), defined the creative industries as "those activities which have their origin and individual creativity, skill and talent and which have a potential for wealth and job creation through the generation and exploitation of intellectual property" (DCMS, 1998 p. 10).[2] After a few years, the first comprehensive analysis of creative activities was undertaken by the UNESCO, with a specific focus on recognizing their role in economic growth: "creative industries have become increasingly important components of modern post-industrial knowledge-based economies. Not only are they thought to account for higher than average growth and job creation, they are also vehicles of cultural identities that play an important role in fostering cultural diversity" (UNESCO, 2006, p. 3). Besides this acknowledgment, the problem of its definition was still present, as the "problem with any investigation of the creative industries is that the term itself is problematic" (Drake, 2003, p. 512). There was no agreement as to where the boundary lies between cultural and creative industries and between other economic activities. Moreover, each country has since developed further specifications that better fit the local situation. In Italy in particular, the more recent definitions of cultural and creative industry will be referenced, the first from 2009, in the *Libro Bianco sulla creatività* (Santagata, 2009). Besides the two main macro-sectors defined by the KEA report (KEA European Affairs, 2006) – "historical heritage and artistic production" and "production of cultural contents, information, and communications" – the macro-sector of "material culture" has also been added, a typically Italian aspect that comprehends not only fashion and design, but even specific kinds of food production and distribution. In the same direction, in Italy, the report *Io sono cultura* (Fondazione Symbola, Unioncamere, 2014) also considers the "production of *creative driven* goods and services", enlarging the field to include an extremely wide variety of activities such as food and wine services, production of pasta, furniture repairs, housing services, manufacture of watches, yachts, doors or windows, just to mention a few.

Even if the field of creative production is still out of focus, what is commonly agreed upon is the growing economic and social role of the creative and cultural industry in the past years. In 2010, the sector contributed 2.6 per cent of the EU GDP and provided quality jobs to about five million people in the 27 EU Member countries. Today, those numbers have increased, with culture and creative sector jobs employing over 6 million people.[3]

In Milan: figures and roots

Creative production in Milan can be defined as selecting specific "creative-related" activities from the more general categories of "Manufacturing activities", "Information and communication services", "Professional, scientific, and technical (architectural and engineering) activities" and "Arts, sports, and entertainment activities" from the last Italian Census of Industry and services available (2011). This approach is one of the possible methods to count them. According to the data, 71,000 local units are active in Milan in the four sectors mentioned above, but those that can be included in the "creative sector" are about 36,000.[4] They, in particular, correspond to the 19 per cent of the total local units, while the same categories in Rome are approximately 41,000 (16 per cent of the total), in Turin, about 12,800 (14.6 per cent of total). In total, the number of local units in Italy is about 578,000 (12 per cent of the total). Furthermore, in terms of the number of employees in creative production in Milan are 128,000 (16.5 per cent); in Rome 152,754 (16 per cent); in Turin 54,338 (15.7 per cent), and in Italy as a whole they are 1,800,000 (9.8 per cent).[5]

The creative and cultural industries in Milan are entrenched in the economy of the city, known both as the "capital of fashion", whose most representative icon is the so called fashion *Quadrilatero* in the city centre (Jansonn and Power, 2010; D'Ovidio, 2008). The city is also known as the "capital of design", displayed especially in the traditional Milan Trade Fair's Furniture Exhibition (first held in 1961) and the related *Fuorisalone* events (established in the 1990s) spread throughout the city (Figure 1.8).

Besides the numbers for creative production, which confirm Milan's leading position in the Italian scene in the field of creative and cultural industry together with Rome, it is worth noticing the highest percentage of local units and employees compared with the total number and the fact that in Milan the establishment of creative activities are "long-term" stories (D'Ovidio, 2015; D'Ovidio and Pradel, 2013). Creative industry, in fact, is deeply rooted in the education and training network (Balducci et al., 2010), and in the strong specialization in advanced services that have rapidly increased in the city in recent decades. Design-related production, in particular, is embedded in the industrial character of the city, with reference to the important manufacturing tradition that has been consolidated over time in the entire Lombardy region. Since the 1950s, the bond between design talent, craft, manufacturing capabilities, and industrial innovation has created partnerships that have shaped the history of Italian and international design, creating worldwide, well-known brands like *Cappellini, Driade, De Padova, Fontanarte, Artemide, Boffi, B & B Italy*, or *Cassina*. Most of these brands developed in relation with a productive environment, characterized by a widespread presence of small- and medium-sized firms and crafts, historically and locally rooted, often organized in productive districts (such as the furniture-wood district in Brianza, located north of Milan), that keep being relevant even though furniture production has been partially delocalized to developing countries.

Creative production spatial concentration and urban regeneration

Localization and reputation

If the "nature" of creative and cultural industries must still be investigated, as well as the criteria to count them, the same can be said for their spatial concentration. According to the principles used to classify creative productions, their typology, dimension, and the consistency can differ.

There are numerous names given by contemporary literature in the international debate to this phenomenon of urban concentration: "creative or cultural district", "creative neighbourhood", "creative or cultural cluster", "creative or cultural milieu". The heterogeneity of such terms reflects the variety of facts and approaches used to analyse them, paying specific attention to the role of artists and/or creative class in producing "naturally occurring" creative districts able to maintain "authenticity". It also concerns the economic dynamics of the creative activities' clustering (Pratt, 2011), or of the industrial districts (Beccattini,1998; Sacco and Ferilli, 2006); the cultural offer and its fruition (Montgomery, 2003, Roodhouse, 2006; Legnér and Ponzini, 2009); the intangible elements able to build a special "atmosphere" or urban buzz (Storper and Venables, 2004), just to mention a few.

However, we consider these aspects within the framework of the knowledge-based economy. With the changing of traditional work, creative production becomes a relevant asset in many Western cities. Moreover, its capability to replace former functions to be adaptable and fill empty or vacant spaces, to be in-between production and consumption, makes this kind of production able to not only change spaces, but also to affect the reputation of neighbourhoods, even more than other specializations.

In Milan, the distribution of publishers, as well as of fashion and design activities, could appear homogeneous and spread in many parts of the city. Nonetheless, some places are known as being "creative" or presenting more "recognizable" concentrations of creative activities than others. That is because, besides the presence of specific functions and activities in specific areas, the status obtained following their presence amplifies the effects of the concentration itself. Hence in Milan, "urban creative concentrations" (Bruzzese, 2015a) are the result of both material and immaterial transformations. Physical interventions on buildings and branding campaigns have often had a relevant role in making the area known as a place of "creative production".

*Recurring elements: spatial conditions/temporary events
and branding*

In Milan, several cases of "urban creative concentrations" can be recognized. Besides their presence in specific areas with a relevant number of creative activities, these concentrations are characterized by both recurring spatial conditions and other qualitative elements related to the reputation and atmosphere of places, often the result of temporary uses and branding activities (Bruzzese, Botti and Giuliani, 2013; Bruzzese, 2015 a, b).

Spatial conditions. At least four recurring spatial conditions are at the base of the concentration of creative productions, and at the starting point of incremental regeneration processes.

- Semi-central position. Several "urban creative concentrations" in Milan are located where, in the first half of the twentieth century, manufacturing firms were established thanks to the proximity to railways and related infrastructural nodes.[6] They are intermediate areas within the Milan municipality, between the historical centre and the outskirts, with apartment rental costs similar to residential areas of a high/medium level.[7]
- Small-medium size buildings. The industrial buildings where creative production is established in Milan is usually in small-medium size buildings (15,000–17,000 sqm) that have lost their original functions since the mid-seventies. The spatial features suit the needs of creative industries, including exhibitions, and can be transformed at relatively affordable costs by private operators.
- Different typologies/mixed-use condition. These buildings are located within an urban fabric where, in the past, production was mixed with residence, services, and trade, in a wide range of spaces and of building typologies. The mixed-use condition, together with the mixed-space offer, definitely assisted the process of replacing previous activities with new and heterogeneous ones.
- Spaces still available. The disposal of former industrial functions occurred in these areas and has left a number of spaces still available for transformation. This has made possible the incremental processes started by the so-called "pioneer interventions".

Reputation and branding. Beside physical and morphological conditions, other aspects have played a relevant role in defining the nature of "creative concentrations" and in feeding the process of urban regeneration inside the

Milan municipal area. They are qualitative and immaterial elements but, all the same, able to affect the perception of place, such as:

- the high reputation of some creative activities established in a specific area (skilled more than others to mobilize interests and attract attention, both at the local and supra-local scale, and somehow to generate a creative environment);
- the overlap between localization of activities and temporary events;
- the use of promotional and place-branding interventions of various kinds, aimed at improving the reputation of places hosting creative industries and events;
- the public status that, in recent years, has put these areas on the mental map of the Milan as "creative places".

These concentrations of creative productions generate a peculiar geography of places and uses. Such geography shows an interesting dynamic between permanent localizations of creative production and temporary localizations of practices linked to the event organization that occurs during *Design Week* or *Fashion Week*[8] (Figure 1.8). The above mentioned *Fuorisalone*, in particular, has the strongest impact on the city both in terms of number of visitors and an ephemeral geography of centralities.[9] It can be defined as the set of initiatives, events, trade fairs, and creative activities that happen in the entire municipal area during the *Design Week*, while the Milan annual *International Furniture Fair* takes place in the new official fairground, between Milan and Rho[10] (Figure 1.8). At the beginning of the 1980s, this spontaneous phenomenon involved only young and emerging designers seeking alternative locations around the city. Year after year, this trend gradually expanded, giving birth in the 1990s to the current event that fills industrial spaces, streets, showrooms, and galleries with initiatives and exhibitions in several Milan districts.

Empirical evidences: creative productions and processes of urban regeneration on going

The features listed on p. 64 occur in different areas of the municipality of Milan, where creative production has been at the base of urban regeneration. One of the most recognized is the *Porta Genova-Tortona area*, located in the south-western part of the city[11] (Figures 1.6 and 1.8). It is a well-known "design-neighbourhood" that, in recent years, has also become the core of the *Fuorisalone*. It is a case of private-driven urban regeneration (Bruzzese, 2015a; Armondi and Bruzzese, 2017), established almost 30 years

66 *Antonella Bruzzese*

ago. During the 1980s, this area was a peripheral neighbourhood outside the city railway belt with plenty of former industrial buildings, abandoned due to phenomena of de-localization and changes in the production system. A group of photographers and fashion operators transformed some of these buildings into the *Superstudio*, a space for photo shoots, exhibitions, and art publishing. This place became a pioneer of intervention that opened to an incremental process of change. Between 1985 and 2015, this process brought about the transformation of 14 industrial buildings from traditional manufacturing to creative activities operated by private entrepreneurs (Bruzzese, 2015a; Giuliani, 2015), including *Esprit, Kenzo, Zegna, Hugo Boss, Gas, Diesel, Tod's*, as well as the *Armani* museum. Here, more than in any other area in Milan, the arrival of creative activities was deeply intertwined with recursive temporary events and initiatives – such as the already mentioned *Fashion Week* and *Design Week* – along with a strong investment in place branding.[12] That combination made the "zone" known as a place of events and pushed the process of replacing old activities with new ones. These include "trendy" restaurants and bars as well as the new *MUDEC* public museum[13] and the *Base* public project hub[14] in the former Ansaldo (Figure 1.6 and 1.8). After three decades since this process began, the *Porta Genova-Tortona* area now contains a mix of different functions; has become a recognized area established with important international brands; vacant buildings and spaces have been almost completely reused; and a process of gentrification, through the replacement of the old population, is ongoing. Nevertheless, the closeness to one of the abandoned railway yards that is planned to be converted for urban uses, could be the impetus for a further step of transformation of the area.

Ventura-Lambrate is a neighbourhood located between the railway belt and the highway belt, in the eastern sector of Milan's municipal area[15] (Figure 1.6 and 1.8). Until the 1970s, it used to be an industrial district with several manufacturing firms, most of them now abandoned or underused. Compared to the *Porta Genova-Tortona* area, it has analogous morphological conditions and a similar urban change process, even if dimensions of the phenomena and stage of the process are quite different. The recovery of *Faema* (the historical industry of coffee machines) in the early 2000s can be considered the pioneer intervention that mobilized a network of actors from Milan's creative industry scene. Here, they found advantages of mutual proximity and skills to promote new business set up in the area as a whole. This paved the way to an urban regeneration process that affirmed the *Ventura-Lambrate* area not only as creative concentration, but also as a "temporary centrality". Even in this case, the *Fuorisalone* played the role as the engine to temporarily reuse abandoned spaces, quite well preserved, suited for exhibitions and concentrated in an area already maintaining the reputation of a "creative quarter" (Bruzzese, 2015a, b). In 2007, a group of Dutch designers in search of spaces, alternative to the ones settled in the *Porta Genova-Tortona* area, took the opportunity to present their projects in one of the on-going construction sites, opening the way to a temporary occupation of spaces that has been repeated in the following years.[16] Beside temporary uses, the regeneration process transformed a limited number of former industrial buildings into lofts, art galleries, and studios, but has had a great impact on the neighbourhood's reputation, now recognized as one of the most dynamic outskirts of the Milan municipal area. This perception is also due to an important network of local associations that, during the same years, promoted several projects of public space activation, somehow animated by the yearly *Fuorisalone*. However, the *Ventura-Lambrate* process seems to be "unfinished". It seems to not have enough strength to actually regenerate the whole area, where there are still former industrial buildings. Several of them are quite large and require massive operations that the current real estate market is not able to absorb (Gingardi, 2017).

Bovisa is another peripheral neighbourhood in the north-western part of Milan with an industrial past and a related strong cultural and social identity (Figure 1.6). After the opening and subsequent enlargement of the Politecnico di Milano's campus[17] (Figure 1.7), which brought many students to the area, a phenomenon of micro-interventions occurred: services for students and bars were set up, together with small-scale creative productions, throughout the whole district. Beyond the university, a public actor able to bring several new users and inhabitants, *Bovisa* has cultural activities and creative productions that grew in the early 2000s. The *Triennale Bovisa*[18] – a temporary cultural exhibition space realized by the real estate operator *Euromilano* – was established in an empty lot and animated the cultural life of the neighbourhood to affirm it as creative place. In parallel, another private-driven intervention, *Base B-Bovisa*, functioned similarly and, together with the recent efforts, has spread temporary *Fuorisalone* events in the neighbourhood. Unfortunately, *Triennale Bovisa* closed for economic reasons, *Base B* was transformed for more traditional functions, and the regeneration of the whole area has not been completely achieved.

The *Porta Romana* district (Figure 1.6 and 1.8), in the southern sector of the Milan municipality, has been "discovered" in the very last years.[19] It is an area beyond the railway in the south of Milan that is characterized by a mix of residential spaces and small productive buildings, many of them now underused. Beside the original spatial conditions (i.e., position, morphological features of the urban fabric, and buildings) that it shares with the other analysed cases, this area is also close to several urban nodes (current or potentials, such as universities, brownfields, as well as the South Milan Agricultural Park[20]). Here, the Fondazione Prada, a private organization and a big brand in both the fashion industry and the cultural scene, has been the pioneer actor for changes to the area's reputation by attracting people and consequently disclosing potentialities in terms of spaces, accessibility, and networks. Interestingly, Fondazione Prada overlaps with local programs promoted by the public administration, aimed at working on smart city issues. Therefore, differently from other cases, there is a sort of concentration of intents from both private and public actors, that could be promising by opening new perspectives.

Finally, *Isola* is an area not as peripheral as the other Milan districts described, and where the presence of former industrial buildings is limited (Figure 1.8). However, this neighbourhood has a strong tradition in craft and commerce, together with a complex story of reaction to the (recently concluded) large project of *Porta Nuova*[21] (Av.Vv, 2013), which has changed the skyline of the whole city. Even if it is different from the others, this case is also interesting to mention as many of its historical craft shops have been replaced by creative productions (such as jewellery, fashion, design), blurring manufacturing with selling. In particular, this case involves a program – promoted by the Milan Municipality and the Lombardy Regional Government – aimed at supporting branding activities and events to promote local attractiveness and identity.[22] Accordingly, creative productions still play an interesting role in preserving the balance between new and large urban change projects (such as *Porta Nuova*), on the one hand, and the heritage of traditional trade and new "crafts", on the other.

Conclusions

The reflection on creative production proposed in this chapter could help to underline some critical nodes and research directions. In Milan, cultural and creative industry has been promoted mainly by private actors. Generally, the processes have not been planned by public actors, so related urban change or innovation projects were unexpected, outside of a public vision or strategy.[23] In the 1990s and in the early 2000s, the role of creative industries as a robust engine for creating jobs and economic growth, as well as tools for promoting cultural diversity and social inclusion, was neither well known nor advocated. Therefore, private players have been the pioneers in Milan.

Current conditions have changed slightly. The approach of Milan's public administration has become more attentive to this issue by promoting several programs and incentives to support different kinds of creative production and new forms of work, often interestingly related to peripheral areas (i.e., the *Sharing Cities* project[24] in the *Porta Romana* area).

The Milan municipal area displays several potentialities, such as the availability of spaces – led by deindustrialization or delocalization processes – and a livelier real estate market. However, interventions able to balance some of the effects led by these transformations – such as processes of expulsion of weaker population, scarcity of synergies with the urban environment, or difficulty to develop regeneration processes in the long run – are necessary. In order to treat them, and to exploit the potentialities of creative production as tools of urban regeneration, public policies need to be improved and promoted (Armondi and Bruzzese, 2017; Mariotti, Pacchi and Di Vita, 2017). They can work at the same time on different fields (i.e., helping the establishment of creative production by providing entrepreneurs with incentives or spaces, preserving the balance between old and new inhabitants and between residents and users, avoiding excessive specialization in functions; improving public space quality, its social animation and interaction with inhabitants, through a stronger collaboration with the private players as well as overcoming the logic of ephemeral and intermittent events, filling the gap between the ordinary daily dimension and the extra-ordinary one). In conclusion, Milan confirms that creative production, and related urban concentrations (here, mainly private-driven), can be the leverage for urban regeneration processes. Nonetheless, without a synergy with public intervention, these regeneration processes can be unfinished, or they can create imbalances that need to be faced, defining a relevant field of intervention for public administrations.

Notes

1 See the EU programme *Creative Europe 2014–2020*.
2 According to this definition, creative industries include: advertising, architecture, the art and antiques market, crafts, design, designer fashion, film and video, interactive leisure software, music, the performing arts, publishing, software and computer services, television and radio.
3 Source: KEA European Affairs, in Fondazione Symbola, Unioncamere, 2014, p. 21.
4 The activities considered are: from "Manufacturing activities" i.e., those related to fashion, furniture and music; from "Information and communication services" the activities of publishing as well as video, cinema, tv, and software related; from "Professional, scientific, and technical (architectural and engineering) activities" those related to architecture, design; from "Arts, sports and entertainment activities" all the activities related to art (Bruzzese, 2015a, p. 17).
5 The data presented here are authors' elaborations from the Italian *Census of Industry* 2011.
6 See Chapter 1.
7 The place where the gentrification effects are more visible is the Porta Genova-Tortona area (Figure 1.8). Here the real estate average price in the period

70 *Antonella Bruzzese*

1993–2012 considerably increased. For example, for "new apartments" it passed from 2.450 €/sq.m to approximately 5.050 €/sq.m (+205 per cent); for "recent apartments (with less than 40 years and refurbished)" from 1.800 to 4.000 (+221 per cent); in the category "apartments, with more than 40 years or to refurbish" from 1.420 to 3.150 (+222 per cent) (OSMI, 2012). Although it appears high, the increase is in line with the trend of Milanese prices in the same period and it is not so different from others registered in neighbouring areas (for example, the homologous data in the near area "Conca del Naviglio" are respectively + 180 per cent; + 190 per cent; + 164 per cent).

8 See Chapter 1.
9 *Fuorisalone* attracted more than 400,000 visitors in the 2016 edition.
10 See Chapter 8.
11 See Chapter 9.
12 The branding campaign to launch the Tortona area started at the beginning of the 2000s.
13 MUDEC is the Museum of Cultures, a centre dedicated to interdisciplinary research on the cultures of the world.
14 Base is a hybrid centre for culture and creativity, assigned *via* public bid by a group of social entrepreneurs.
15 See also Chapter 9.
16 In the *Ventura-Lambrate* area, the events handled by the company Organisation in Design, rose from 22 in 2010 to 176 in 2015; the square meters used for temporary exhibitions and events increased from 5,000 in 2010 to 13,000 in 2015, visitors from 30,000 to more than 100,000.
17 See Chapter 8.
18 Connected to the Milan Triennale, one of the main cultural institutions of the city.
19 See Chapter 6.
20 See Chapter 9.
21 See Chapter 8.
22 For instance, the project *Isola e le sue piazze* (Bruzzese, Gerosa and Tamini, 2016).
23 See Chapters 8 and 10.
24 See Chapter 6.

References

Aa.Vv. (2013). *Fight-specific isola art, architecture, activism and the future of the city*. New York: Archive books.
Armondi, S. and Bruzzese, A. (2017). Contemporary production and urban: The case of Milano. *Journal of Urban Technology*.
Balducci, A., Cognetti F., Fedeli V. eds., (2010). *Milano, la città degli studi. Storia, geografia e politiche delle università milanesi*, Abitare Segesta Cataloghi Collana AIM, Milano.
Becattini, G. (1998). *Distretti industriali e made in Italy*. Torino: Bollati Boringhieri.
Bruzzese, A. (2015a) *Addensamenti creativi, trasformazioni urbane e Fuorisalone*. Maggioli, Rimini.
Bruzzese, A. (2015b). *The places of creative production: Concentrations, features and urban transformation processes in Milan*. Paper presented at the Annual

Meeting on Cultural Heritage 4th Conference, *Cultural creative industries: Economic development and urban regeneration*, Rome.

Bruzzese, A. C., Botti, I. and Giuliani, I. (2013). Territorial branding strategies behind and beyond visions of urbanity: The role of the Fuorisalone event in Milan. *Planum: The Journal of Urbanism*, 28, p. 2.

Bruzzese, A., Gerosa, G. and Tamini, L. (2016). *Spazio pubblico e attrattività urbana: L'isola e le sue piazze*. Milano: Bruno Mondadori.

Camera di Commercio di Milano (Chamber of Commerce of Milan). (2015). *Milano Produttiva 2015*. Milano: Bruno Mondadori.

D'Ovidio, M. (2008). "Tessuti sociali. Relazioni, spazio, creatività nell'industria della moda a Milano", *AIS Giovani Sociologi*, ScriptaWeb, Napoli, pp. 147–166.

D'Ovidio, M. (2015). The field of fashion production in Milan: A theoretical discussion and an empirical investigation. *City, Culture and Society*, 2, p. 6.

D'Ovidio, M. and Pradel, M. (2013). Social innovation and institutionalisation in the cognitive-cultural economy: Two contrasting experiences from Southern Europe. *Cities*, 33, pp. 69–76.

Department for Culture, Media and Sport (DCMS). (1998). *Creative industries mapping*. London: GOV.UK.

Drake, G. (2003). This place gives me space: Place and creativity in the creative industry. *Geoforum*, 34(4), pp. 511–524.

Fondazione Symbola and Unioncamere. (2011). L'Italia che verrà. Industria culturale, made in Italy e territori. *I quaderni di Symbola*.

Fondazione Symbola, Unioncamere. (2014). *Io sono cultura – l'Italia della qualità e della bellezza sfida e della bellezza sfida la crisi*, Report.

Gingardi, V. (2017). Processi di trasformazione urbana a Milano: il caso di Lambrate. *ASUR*, n.118/2017.

Giuliani, I. (2015). *The formation of new urban identities behind and beyond the concentrations of creative and cultural activities. The cases of Long Island city in New York and Zona Tortona in Milan*, Politecnico di Milano, Dipartimento di Architettura e Studi Urbani, Doctoral program in Spatial Planning and Urban Development: doctoral thesis.

Ingallina, P. ed. (2010). *Nuovi scenari per l'attrattivita` delle citta` e dei territori: Dibattiti, progetti e strategie in contesti metropolitani mondiali*. Milano: Franco Angeli.

Jansson, J. and Power, D. (2010). Fashioning a global city: Global city brand channels in the fashion and design industries. *Regional Studies*, 44(7), pp. 889–904.

KEA European Affairs. (2006). *The economy of culture in Europe*. Brussels: European Commission Directorate General for Education and Culture.

Legnér, M. and Ponzini, D. eds. (2009). *Cultural quarters and urban transformation: International perspectives*. Klintehamn: Gotlandica förlag.

Mariotti, I., Pacchi, C. and Di Vita, S. (2017). Coworking spaces in Milan: Location patterns and urban effects. *Journal of Urban Technology*.

Montgomery, J. (2003). Cultural quarters as mechanisms for urban regeneration. Part 1: Conceptualising cultural quarters. *Planning Practice and Research*, 18(4), pp. 293–306.

Neff, G. (2005). The changing place of cultural production: The location of social networks in a digital media industry. *Annals of the American Association of Political and Social Science*, 597(1), pp. 134–152.

72 *Antonella Bruzzese*

Osmi Borsa Milano (2012). 2° Rapporto congiunturale previsionale del mercato immobiliare, Milano.
Pratt, A.C. (2011). "The cultural contradictions of the creative city", *City, Culture and Society*, 2, pp. 123–130.
Roodhouse, S. (2006). *Cultural quarters: Principles and practices*. Bristol: Intellect.
Sacco, P.L. and Ferilli, G. (2006). Il distretto culturale evoluto nell'economia postindustriale. *Working Paper DADI, IUAV* 4:06, Venezia.
Santagata, W. (2009). *Libro Bianco sulla creatività: Per un modello italiano di sviluppo*. Milano: Egea.
Scott, A.J. (2000). *The cultural economy of cities: Essays on the geography of image-producing industries*. London, Thousand Oaks: Sage.
Storper, M. and Venables, A.J. (2004). Buzz: Face-to-face contact and the urban economy. *Journal of Economic Geography*, 4(4), pp. 351–370.
UNESCO. (2006). *Understanding creative industries: Cultural statistics for public-policy making*. Paris. Available at: http://portal.unesco.org/culture/es/files/30297/11942616973cultural_stat_EN.pdf/cultural_stat_EN.pdf.

5 Sharing economy

Makerspaces, co-working spaces, hybrid workplaces, and new social practices

Carolina Pacchi

Introduction

After the crisis of traditional industrial cities and the diffused de-industrialization processes, which took place in Europe and North America in the 1970s and 1980s, signs of a new relationship between urban spaces and forms of production are now emerging. Compared to the location of production sites in urban areas in the twentieth century, the determinants of contemporary phenomena are more strictly connected to the centrality of knowledge: "For its part, knowledge has a tendency to grow indefinitely, for it can be endlessly re-used, is extremely leaky (and hence its circle of users continually expands), and can be combined and recombined in virtually unlimited ways" (Storper and Scott, 2009, p. 148). At the same time, a distinctly social and relational approach to new urban economies is growing (Bolocan Goldstein, 2014). The diffusion of new workspaces, such as co-working spaces or FabLabs, can be connected to these trends, in that they are places of knowledge concentration, production and exchange, clearly based on relational and collaborative dimensions.

A number of trends contribute to shape this relational and social approach in new urban production. Among them, a sharing turn in economic processes is raising and spreading. This can be interpreted more radically as a revolution – able to undermine the global capitalistic economy and to substitute it, step by step, with production and consumption modes based on horizontal relationships and solidarity (Rifkin, 2014) – or as the diffusion of initiatives based on sharing practices, but working firmly within the boundaries of a traditional market economy. Moreover, while the extreme diffusion of means of production (P2P Foundation, 2012) may potentially lead to a more "democratic" attitude of market or quasi-market exchanges, at the same time, the extreme concentration in the hands of a few oligarchic market operators of decision making power ultimately gives them the ability to appropriate value extracted from networks and relationships.

74 *Carolina Pacchi*

The sharing turns seems to be one of the drivers for the location of new workspaces in urban environments, together with the growing relevance of cultural and creative productions in cities (Florida, 2002, 2004; Scott, 2014) and the diffusion of highly skilled freelancers, seen as a strongly innovative, but at the same time precarious and fragile segment of the job market (Allegri and Ciccarelli, 2013; Moriset, 2014). This chapter aims at investigating the possible relationships between more relational, social, and solidarity-based production and consumption models and the role of the urban environment, looking in particular at the Milan case.

Cities are in a good position to become test-beds for the experimentation of new forms of exchange of goods and services for two different types of reasons. They are places in which the most negative impacts of economic globalization in contemporary societies, such as growing inequalities, are most concentrated and accelerated, and therefore forms of social and spatial segregation are most visible and deeply felt (Sassen, 2012; Cucca and Ranci, 2016). Nevertheless, at the same time, they are characterized by density, proximity and diversity, which create an ideal context for sharing practices and to foster and nurture new collaborative social and economic trends.

Today, even continental European cities, traditionally characterized by a significant diffusion of local welfare (Kazepov, 2004), find themselves exposed to growing inequalities and to phenomena similar to those taking place in other regions of the world (MacCallum et al., 2009; Ranci, Brandsen and Sabatinelli, 2014). Therefore they are becoming places of innovation and experimentation of new and more collaborative models for the production and distribution of goods and services, blurring the distinction between producers and users and ultimately redesigning accessibility patterns.

Milan: transformation of the urban environment and diffusion of new workspaces

Looking at Milan, the sharing turn has influenced the diffusion of new workspaces in the city, due to a number of contextual reasons. After the deindustrialization phase, which took place in the 1970s and 1980s, the city has shown a significant degree of resilience, with the persisting diversity of economic sectors and the resistance of a significant quota of manufacturing industry, in particular in the urban region, outside the urban core (Figure 1.4) (OECD, 2006; Ranci, 2009; Balducci, Fedeli and Pasqui, 2011). These two phenomena, combined, have contributed to boost the Milan resilience and to limit job loss. In the years between the 1990s and the explosion of the economic crisis in 2008, the city has maintained a (weak) growth trend (Cucca and Ranci, 2016). In the absence of an identifiable economic development strategy, and of a recognisable public agenda on these topics, Milan has confirmed its reputation as a polyarchic and complex city, not linked to just one centre of power, in which governance coalitions have always been complex, multi-layered and multi-faceted, within and outside the public administration (Dente, Bobbio and Spada, 2005). Creative and cultural productions have been gaining ground as a relevant urban development factor, visible in terms of economic activities, jobs, and urban and physical transformation of parts of the city, together with other sectorial specializations (such as finance, banking, and insurance). As far as jobs are concerned, in 2011 the creative jobs in Milan amounted to 128.000, which is 16.5 per cent of the total jobs (Bruzzese, 2015, pp. 16–17).

The urban growth trend has been changing with the explosion of the crisis, which has hit Italy hard in general, also due to the weakness of its economy, but has also hit, to a lesser extent, the Milan urban region. The crisis has contributed to modify and re-shape production spaces and to trigger the diffusion of innovative workspaces, able to cater for the needs of an emerging constellation of knowledge workers. We can interpret the emerging trend towards the diffusion of new workspaces also as the matching between a new, young and highly skilled workforce in search for a place in society, and the presence of underused physical spaces in search for appropriate reuses. The changed attitude of Local Government towards the support of these emerging trends[1] can be interpreted at the same time as a way to support cutting edge entrepreneurship, in particular in the creative and cultural sector, and as a way to support a fragile young urban population, who live precarious professional lives even in the face of high skills and education.

In Milan, in the last few years, it is possible to notice a wide variety of workspaces which experiment new ways of connecting production processes to forms of horizontal exchange, solidarity, and community building, even if the interpretation of such trends should be critically analysed and discussed (Pacchi, 2015; Mariotti, Pacchi and Di Vita, 2017). Among them, co-working spaces, makerspaces, and hybrid creative and cultural production spaces – frequently located in existing abandoned industrial or public facility buildings – can be identified (Figure 1.8).

Hybrid spaces host a mix of consumption and production, usually in the creative and cultural field. Makerspaces are places in which people meet to make things (Anderson, 2012). Among them, in the last few years, there has been a growing diffusion of FabLabs, which are mainly devoted to digital fabrication and experimentation (Gershenfeld, 2005). Finally, in a general sense, co-working spaces can be defined as "shared workplaces utilised by different sorts of knowledge professionals, mostly freelancers, working in various degrees of specialisation in the vast domain of the knowledge industry" (Gandini, 2015, p. 194). This definition does not describe a specific typology of socio-spatial organization, but it includes a variety of spatial arrangements hosting knowledgable professionals, mainly acting as freelancers in creative and cultural, digital, and social economy sectors.

As co-working spaces are standing out in terms of numbers, visibility and presence in public debates (Spinuzzi, 2012; Capdevila, 2014; Moriset, 2014; Parrino, 2015; Ivaldi and Scaratti, 2015; Waters-Lynch et al., 2016), this chapter mainly focuses on them. In the absence of a shared and codified definition of what a co-working space exactly is, it is difficult to make reliable estimates about the real figures, but it is possible to see quick growth trends of such spaces in Milan, even if they are very different in terms of dimension, location, sectorial specialization.

Such spaces can be exclusively devoted to co-working or they can be a combination of co-working together with a more traditional firm or professional practice, in the need to downsize and share its space. They can be very small, hosting five to ten workplaces, or extremely large, hosting more than one hundred people, representing individual professionals and freelancers, as well as small firms, start-ups, or otherwise. In some cases, co-working is one of the activities in hybrid centres, devoted more in general to creative and cultural production and, therefore, also hosting spaces for exhibitions, art performances, or artist residences.

In the Italian context, the life of such professionals can be extremely precarious and difficult (Allegri and Ciccarelli, 2013). In this sense, the option of working in such spaces can be seen as a coping strategy for people facing very hard labour market dynamics, also due to the absence of traditional forms of political representation (Colleoni and Arvidsson, 2014; Gandini, 2016). These professionals, who trade security for freedom (Parrino, 2015), need new places to share with others the difficulties and loneliness implicit in their professional life.

Milan is the Italian city in which the presence of such new socio-spatial arrangements for shared workspaces is more diffused (MyCowo, 2014; Coworking Italia, 2014) – with estimates between 80 and 100 spaces in 2016, for a population of around 1000 co-workers – and in which this trend has influenced both new workspaces and existing, more or less traditional workspaces, frequently transformed and given new meaning in the last few years (Mariotti, Pacchi and Di Vita, 2017).

The main reasons for the quick diffusion of co-working spaces are generally connected to the possibility of knowledge exchange, community building and cooperation thanks to proximity among workers and, to a lesser extent, to emerging needs for places of representation for traditionally non-represented knowledge professionals. The results of a field-research on co-working spaces in Milan (Pacchi, 2015) highlighted that, in the perception of co-working managers, the first question is of paramount importance. Many researches do in fact show how knowledge exchange, in particular as far as tacit knowledge is concerned, is a crucial feature of such spaces: "Just by belonging to a local community, an insider will have access to the shared knowledge among members of similar but distant communities" (Capdevila, 2014, p. 2). Networking and community building are also relevant features: co-workers tend to rely on connections they establish in co-working spaces to enlarge their professional networks, to get in contact with new clients, and to build more complex projects, exploiting a multi-professional technical expertise. As a matter of fact, many co-workers clearly express their satisfaction and appreciate the possibilities shared environments offer them to strengthen personal relationships and to overcome loneliness (that is usual for home workers). The empirical research in Milan tends to confirm evidence from literature (Spinuzzi, 2012; Capdevila, 2014; Parrino, 2015), in particular as far as the knowledge spill-over and the sharing atmosphere are concerned, even if tensions between cooperation and competition, as well as between inclusive and exclusive environments demand for further investigation.

The possibility to get together and build a political "voice" is more critical: in Milan, co-working managers underline the basic individuality of these workers, their scant engagement in building new forms of political representation (even in the face of widely diffused low income, precariousness, lack of social security), and the difficulty for co-working spaces to also become spaces of political or even just professional representation. We will discuss this again in the final part of this chapter.

Looking at their spatial distribution in Milan (Mariotti, Di Vita and Limonta, 2015; Mariotti, Pacchi and Di Vita, 2017), co-working spaces are unevenly located in the urban region, and in particular there is a significant concentration in the urban core (Figure 1.8). In the central city, corresponding to the boundaries of the Milan Municipality, co-working spaces are concentrated in three areas: one corresponding to the Isola-Porta Nuova-Sarpi district, a former working class and mixed-function area, largely gentrified in the last twenty years[2]; the second one is the Porta Genova-Tortona area, a former industrial area between the two main Navigli, in the Southern part of the city, which has been transformed into a creative and cultural district for at least twenty years (Bruzzese, 2015); and finally, a third recognisable cluster is located in the North-East part of the city, corresponding to a number of traditional working class and small industry neighbourhoods which are still on the way of urban and economic restructuring (Ventura-Lambrate, Loreto, viale Monza-via Padova-Ponte Nuovo). Co-working locations in other parts of the city are more sporadic (for instance in Porta Romana-Bocconi area) and their effects are therefore not so significant, or still in a nascent phase.[3]

The geography of makerspaces tends to be very similar, with the notable difference that they are located primarily in former industrial spaces, while co-working spaces are more flexible, as they can occupy former tertiary or residential units.

Hybrid spaces need larger premises for their development, because their model revolves around combination and contamination between different functions, such as cultural and art productions, entertainment, co-working, fostering entrepreneurship, and the promotion of social inclusion; therefore, they tend to occupy former industrial buildings or abandoned public facilities in different areas of the city.

The interpretation of this spatial distribution can be put in relation to different types of reasons: one has to do with very traditional location determinants, such as real estate market prices and accessibility (in particular via public transportation); other, more contextual explanations, can be proposed to specifically connect the emergence of spaces for co-working (together with makerspaces and hybrid cultural spaces) to the changing features of different neighbourhoods. The individual processes of urban transformation and regeneration, coupled with inevitable gentrification effects, influence locational choices in particular when cultural and creative districts are in formation, in different stages of their evolution.

In such cases, co-working spaces are not the pioneers, other more consolidated actors in the knowledge economy have been the first to locate in changing neighbourhoods, and co-workings or makerspaces follow. In a couple of cases, such as viale Monza-via Padova, on the contrary, such spaces appear to have been pioneers, the first to locate, in previously abandoned neighbourhoods or in areas still characterized by the presence of very traditional urban functional mixes, residential and small tertiary or manufacturing activities, residential and local retail. It thus becomes useful to understand in which cases and under which conditions new workspaces can play a pioneering role and become themselves the initiators of larger and more complex processes of urban transformation (Zukin and Braslow, 2011).

Looking at individual cases of co-working spaces, is possible to mention two very different examples: the first are the two co-working spaces of the *Talent Garden* network open in Milan; the second is the multifunctional space of *Open*, hosting a co-working space jointly with a bookstore and a café.

Talent Garden (TAG) is an international network of co-working spaces aimed at digital workers now present in five European countries with seventeen spaces (Waters-Lynch et al., 2016; www.talentgarden.org); since the target is digital productions, TAG selects people according to their field of specialization, and offers them international connections in these fields; the first space in Milan was opened up in 2011, in the North-East area neighbouring Viale Monza,[4] and today it hosts around 140 people including freelancers, start-ups, and small firms, in 1,500 sqm equipped with shared services and characterized by a very dynamic programme of activities aimed at connecting people, strengthening network opportunities and knowledge exchange. A second, much larger co-working space has been opened in South East Milan in 2015,[5] an area still in the process of transformation from an industrial and working class neighbourhood into an area characterized by creative and cultural activities and by the presence of large international firms. This second space, which will be able to host more than 400 co-workers in 8,000 sqm shares the basic service of the TAG network, offering additional facilities such as a café, a swimming pool, and gardens. The TAG co-working spaces are a good example of very effective spaces, extremely active in the creation and maintenance of a community, both on site and internationally, and it is one of the few cases in Italy of very large co-working spaces, which are already the trend in other parts of the world; at the same time, the creation of a strong internal community does not always correspond to forms of embeddedness at local level, in particular as far as neighbourhood effects are concerned.

A quite different example is *Open – More than Books* (www.openmilano. com), a mixed space for culture, leisure, and work located in Porta Romana (Figure 1.8), in a very dense and compact neighbourhood bordering the city centre. In this case, this mixed function space, open in 2013, hosts co-working places (40 places, on a permanent and on a daily basis), spaces for students, a café and bistro, and a bookstore, which in turn organizes events, books presentations, conferences, and so on. A mix of functions, able to bring very diverse people to meet in this space, with blurred boundaries among the different areas/activities and entertaining a quite strong relationship with the surrounding neighbourhood. In this case, co-working is not an exclusive activity, because the space is designed with an idea of community building though contamination. The diversity of the examples which have been described is a very good representation of the diversity of the conceptions of co-working as an activity, and therefore as a socio-spatial configuration, which have been diffusing in Milan in recent years.

Looking at hybrid spaces, some recent cases in Milan are:

* Santeria Social Club, a 1,000 sqm space located in a former car dealer, and BASE Milano, a 6,000 sqm hybrid space located in a former engine and train production factory (both in the Porta Genova-Tortona area) (Figure 1.8);
* Mare Milano, a 7,000 sqm former rural farmstead in the Western periphery of the city.

These three examples are particularly interesting because they are the first results of a policy initiated by the Municipality after 2014 for the reuse of abandoned buildings for social and cultural purposes, which led to experimenting with new forms of interface between the public administration and local grassroots or private actors. In parallel with this policy, the Municipality actively worked to support the diffusion and strengthening of co-working spaces, as places fostering the knowledge economy, through a system of incentives both on the supply and on the demand side (Comune di Milano, 2014).

Conclusion

The diffusion of new workspaces, in their different socio-spatial arrangements, sizes, and locations, highlights a deep change in the relationship between forms of production, urban space, and local societies. Even if still a niche phenomenon, it contains some signs of a new approach to this complex relationship. We can summarize the main emerging features for future discussion in two main questions: one is political and it touches upon the relationship between knowledgeable professionals and job market dynamics, the second has more to do with the dynamics of urban space in its dichotomic nature of space of flows/space of places (Castells, 2009).

The first question is *political*: in the face of ever increasing social inequalities and social and spatial segregation of fragile populations in contemporary cities, such spaces do not act as places of political representation, but simply as places aimed at hosting new fragile and precarious, even if highly skilled, workers and at giving visibility to their (personal, social, political) needs. This aspect is strictly related to the knowledge professions, and with the need to more precisely investigate to which extent the weakness of these professionals in the Italian context can be (partially) compensated by the reliance on sharing and horizontal exchange practices (at the micro level of the workspace, but also more generally at the urban level), in order to understand if this will enable them to overcome their traditional fragility in a hard labour market and therefore to fully exploit their potential in terms of local development (Allegri and Ciccarelli, 2013). In this sense, there is the risk that the hype on the sharing dimension might overshadow increasing social and economic inequalities, rather than becoming a possible answer. Here the tensions between inclusivity (as the opportunity for such workers to be included in dense networks for sharing knowledge and building new professional opportunities) and exclusivity (as the risk of the creation of "bubbles" secluded from the urban space), and between cooperation and competition within these "bubbles" can help to more precisely highlight and understand the underlying dynamics.

The second question is specifically urban, in that it is not yet clear which will be the ability of these workspaces to positively impact urban spaces outside of their strict boundaries, or to diffuse practices and initiatives of sharing, community building, and knowledge exchange, and conversely, which will be the ability of urban decision makers to fully exploit the potential of these workspaces and to socialize their effects (particularly important in the light of the public support they have been receiving, which puts in question the publicness of their impacts).

As we have also seen in the Milan case, these spaces seem to be better inserted into spaces of flows, offering to their users opportunities to be connected in long range international networks, than in spaces of places, frequently showing a weakness in fully becoming local players at neighbourhood and/or urban level. To deepen this reflection, we can identify different typologies of new workspaces, some more interested to involve a diverse range of communities (hybrid spaces are a good example, in that they tend to host co-workers, freelancers, start-ups together with artists, citizens, local actors), others more focused on sectorial groups, such as co-workers in the strict sense. In the Milan case, it clearly emerges that only the more hybrid workspaces tend to have a degree of openness to the city, and thus to become urban actors; spaces exclusively devoted to co-working, be they small, office-like facilities offering just a few workplaces, or be they very large, organized and networked spaces, are very rarely able to play this role, either because this is not their main mission, or because they do not have the resources to do so. This in turns opens up a reflection on the appropriateness of different forms of public support, which should be aimed at both supporting the career paths of more fragile workers, but at the same time to foster and diffuse urban transformation effects.

Lastly, the huge differentiation among such spaces and the fact that significant (public and private) experimentation is still underway in their definition, set up, and management, makes it difficult to understand if and in what measure they are able to respond to the effects of the economic crisis, and to offer alternative paths to foster local economic development, through the circulation of relational and interaction resources.

Notes

1 See Chapter 10.
2 See Chapter 8.
3 See Chapter 6.
4 See also Chapter 7.
5 See Chapter 6.

References

Allegri, G. and Ciccarelli, R. (2013). *Il quinto stato. Perché il lavoro indipendente è il nostro futuro: Precari, autonomi, free-lance per una nuova società*. Milano: Ponte alle Grazie.

Anderson, C. (2012). *Makers: The new industrial revolution.* New York: Random House Business Books.

Balducci, A., Fedeli, V. and Pasqui, G. eds. (2011). *Strategic planning for contemporary urban regions.* London: Ashgate.

Bolocan, M. (2014). Geografie newyorkesi, ripensando Milano. *Imprese & Città,* 3, pp. 90–95.

Bruzzese, A. (2015). *Addensamenti creative, trasformazioni urbane e Fuorisalone: Casi milanesi tra riqualificazione fisica e trasformazione di immagine.* Sant'Arcangelo di Romagna: Maggioli.

Capdevila, I. (2014). Coworking spaces and the localized dynamics of innovation: The case of Barcelona. *Working Paper.*

Castells, M. (2009). *The rise of the network society.* Volume I, Second edition with a new preface, Oxford: Wiley-Blackwell.

Colleoni, E. and Arvidsson, A. (2014). *Metodi di acquisizione e riconoscimento delle skills informali dei giovani nell'economia della conoscenza di Milano: Il ruolo dei co-working spaces a Milano,* Mimeo.

Comune di Milano. (2014). *Milano sharing city,* Linee di Indirizzo.

Coworking Italia. (2014). *Coworking a Milano,* Infographic, December. Available at: http://coworkingitalia.org/i-coworking-a-milano-eccoli-in-uninfografica-di-co working-italia/.

Cucca, R. and Ranci, C. (2016). *Unequal cities: The challenge of post-industrial transition in times of austerity.* London, New York: Routledge.

Dente, B., Bobbio, L. and Spada, A. (2005). A tale of two cities. *DISP the Planning Review,* 162, pp. 41–52.

Florida, R. (2002). *The rise of the creative class.* New York: Basic Books.

Florida, R. (2004). *Cities and the creative class.* London: Routledge.

Gandini, A. (2015). The rise of coworking spaces: A literature review. *Ephemera: Theory and Politics in Organization,* 15(1), pp. 193–205.

Gandini, A. (2016). *The reputation economy: Understanding knowledge work in digital society.* London: Palgrave MacMillan.

Gershenfeld, N. (2005). *Fab: The coming revolution on your desktop – From personal computers to personal fabrication.* New York: Basic Books.

Ivaldi, S. and Scaratti, G. (2015). *Co-working spaces: Typologies and relevant features,* paper presented to the 9th International Conference on Researching Work and Learning, Singapore, December.

Kazepov, Y. ed. (2004). *Cities of Europe: Changing contexts, local arrangement and the challenge to urban cohesion.* Hoboken: Wiley-Blackwell.

MacCallum, D., Moulaert, F., Hillier, J. and Vicari, S. eds. (2009). *Social innovation and territorial development.* Farnham: Ashgate.

Mariotti, I., Di Vita, S. and Limonta, G. (2015). Una geografia degli spazi di coworking a Milano. *Imprese & Città,* 8, pp. 72–80.

Mariotti, I., Pacchi, C. and Di Vita, S. (2017). Coworking spaces in Milan: Location patterns and urban effects. *Journal of Urban Technology,* published online 25 May 2017.

Moriset, B. (2014). *Building new places of the creative economy: The rise of coworking spaces*. paper presented at the 2nd Geography of Innovation International Conference, Utrecht.

MyCowo. (2014). *Infografica sul coworking in Italia*. Available at: http://mycowo.com/wp-content/uploads/2014/07/infografica-coworking-italia.png.

OECD. (2006). *Territorial review: Milan*. Paris. Available at: www.oecd.org/italy/oecdterritorialreviewsmilanitaly.htm.

P2P Foundation. (2012). *Synthetic overview of the collaborative economy*, Report.

Pacchi, C. (2015). Coworking e innovazione urbana a Milano. *Imprese & Città*, 8, pp. 89–95.

Parrino, L. (2015). Coworking: Assessing the role of proximity in knowledge exchange. *Knowledge Management Research & Practice*, 13, pp. 261–271.

Ranci, C. ed. (2009). *Milano e le città d'Europa tra competitività e disuguaglianze*. Santarcangelo di Romagna: Maggioli.

Ranci, C., Brandsen, T. and Sabatinelli, S. eds. (2014). *Social vulnerability in European cities: The role of local welfare in times of crisis*. London: Palgrave Macmillan.

Rifkin, J. (2014). *The zero marginal cost society: The internet of things, the collaborative commons, and the eclipse of capitalism*. London: Palgrave Macmillan.

Sassen, S. (2012). *Cities in a world economy*. Thousand Oaks: Pine Forge Press (or. Ed. 1994).

Scott, A.J. (2014). Beyond the creative city: Cognitive – Cultural capitalism and the new urbanism. *Regional Studies*, 48(4), pp. 565–578.

Spinuzzi, C. (2012).Working alone, together: Coworking as emergent collaborative activity. *Journal of Business and Technical Communication*, 26(4), pp. 399–441.

Storper, M. and Scott, A. (2009). Rethinking human capital, creativity and urban growth. *Journal of Economic Geography*, 9, pp. 147–167.

Waters-Lynch, J., Potts, J., Butcher, T., Dodson, J. and Hurley, J. (2016). Coworking: A transdisciplinary overview. *Working Paper*, February.

Zukin, S. and Braslow, L. (2011). The life cycle of New York's creative districts: Reflections on the unanticipated consequences of unplanned cultural zones. *City, Culture and Society*, 2, pp. 131–140.

6 Forms of urban change

Nodes of knowledge-based networks as drivers of new metropolitan patterns in Southern Milan

Corinna Morandi and Mario Paris

Introduction

The image of "explosion of the city" (Font, 2007) describes the sprawl process of consolidated European cities within a larger area (Soja, 2011a) and its impacts on contemporary post-metropolitan territories (Soja, 2011b; Knox, 2008). Due to this process, several functions traditionally located in city centres have moved to urban fringes. This movement relies on ambiguous dynamics, where dispersion and concentration coexist, generating original spatial figures (Pavia, 2002; Secchi, 1994; Genette, 1992). During the last ten years, this territorial paradigm has required alternative interpretative frameworks, at times radically different to those currently shared by academia (Portas, Domingues and Cabral, 2011). One approach relies on the updated conceptualization of territorial networks and nodes, both physical and immaterial, in describing territorial dynamics. Accordingly, this chapter focuses on different nodes of knowledge-based networks located in the southern area of the Milan urban region, pointing out (i) their – sometime potential – role as re-activators of metropolitan contexts and (ii) their identity based on the specific quality of urbanity they provide, while also taking into account their different scales.

Southern Milan: a peculiar context within the urban region

This section highlights some specific conditions (e.g., urban patterns and morphologies, concentration and scattering of functions, land uses, presence of innovative and "traditional" activities, role of infrastructures in terms of connection and separation, as well as interscalarity) and constraints (i.e., *Parco agricolo sud* and physical barriers) of a paradigmatic field of analysis. This is the southern sector of the Milan urban region, as it results at the end of the historical process of urban growth, also through the annexation of neighbouring municipalities. This process was both supported and accelerated by the progressive de-centralization of specialized services and innovative functions. For instance, Southern Milan hosts several research and higher-education venues, such as the Università Bocconi, Università IULM, NABA Academy, Domus Academy, IFOM,[1] and IEO[2] (Figure 1.7). Furthermore, this area shows evidence for the repositioning process of economic assets following the crisis, with different trends and levels of importance (De las Rivas and Paris, 2013). To explore this statement, the theoretical frame refers to territorial networks and nodes.

In the southern area of the Milan urban region, the mass urbanization has for a long time been partly prevented by the economic importance of agriculture, which has contributed to some extraordinary features of this unique environment: the water system, made by the *Navigli* with a dense and efficient network of canals for irrigation, villas and traditional farms (*cascine*). The metropolitan scale of the *Parco Agricolo Sud Milano* (Figure 1.3) has been pivotal, always performing the dual tasks of maintaining both the economic and environmental role of agriculture. The intense land transformations have occurred during phases of high pressure by the real estate market. Negotiations between major developers and local governments of small municipalities resulted in the current and peculiar character of the area. The superposition of new infrastructures on the historical territorial pattern has supported the creation of "isles" of new activities that, though compact and often gated, are close to former small urban centres that have massively "exploded". Commercial platforms, logistics, and residential settlements served as pioneers of urbanization, in continuous economic and spatial competition with agriculture and, in few cases, with metropolitan scale facilities.

Southern Milan has been characterized by two major territorial sections. On one hand, the south-western section contains important environmental features. The canal system of the Navigli, which historically provided transport of goods and water for manufacturing and irrigation, now also functions as a touristic hotspot. A recent road axis (Nuova Vigevanese) runs west, parallel to the Naviglio Grande, shaping the major commercial strip of the urban region. Other main roads run south, dotted by huge monofunctional isles, with the exception being the complex node of Assago-Milanofiori (Figures 1.6 and 1.7). Recent trends show the still relevant role of agriculture, in part due to the recent growth of slow tourism, while some indicators reveal a decrease in the consolidated presence of logistics and large scale retail.

On the other hand, the south-eastern area is characterized by the most relevant infrastructures at the national scale: from the historical via Emilia, to motorway, railway, and high-speed railway to Southern Italy. They have been drivers of industrial development, but they are also barriers for both east-west and north-south relations. This role of infrastructures is specifically evident for the Milan Porta Romana railway yard[3] (Figure 1.6), formerly a powerful attractor of industries. Today, it is caught between the compact city to the north and the dense, but porous fabric to the south that is undergoing a deep process of urban change. Here, in recent decades, the process of de-industrialization and service metamorphosis involved both the main city periphery and the first ring of surrounding municipalities, with manufacturing and logistical clusters still in operation near the Milan Rogoredo railway yard. An intense and fast transformation oriented to knowledge economy emerges in the "triangle" defined by via Emilia and via Ripamonti. This area hosts a cluster of initiatives related to the Milan Smart City program, where new spaces dedicated to digital fabrication also appear. This regeneration process is currently branded by the recent Fondazione Prada art gallery and museum (Figure 1.8), performing as a knowledge-based node. Developed by a private actor – which took advantage of the opportunity to transform a private area (before used as a warehouse and temporary exhibition space) – it represents just one fragment of a larger urban change process involving the entire neighbourhood. The Fondazione Prada – that sits nearby a major former industrial site, redeveloped in the 1990s as part of a mix-used neighbourhood – is (probably) acting as a driver of urban regeneration. After its opening, several interventions have been replacing other dismissed factories with tertiary businesses and services,[4] besides houses.

Nodes of knowledge-based network?

Over the last three decades, Western countries have experienced relevant changes related to socio-economic trends, technological innovation, and transformation within governance approaches. In several European cities, a metropolitan de-localization of activities (such as specialized retail, entertainment and cultural facilities, public and private services, innovative and elitist manufacturing) has characterized the urban cores. This transformation has relied not only on public investments in new infrastructures, but also on strategies of private stakeholders, which share the opportunities represented by both the demand generated by dense urban systems and the metropolitan attraction of external users. In some cases, the result reveals an overlay of different and interacting phenomena: the *technoburb* of Fishman (1987), the *edge city* of Garreau (1992) or the *metapolis* of Ascher (1995), adapted to local constraints and contemporary trends. Within this original European context, some different elements, more than others, affect the spatial characteristics of a site and the everyday life of its inhabitants. Amongst others, the "territorial nodes" arise as figures useful to frame the interaction between digital and material networks (Morandi, Rolando and Di Vita, 2016) and the role of different flows (of people, goods, and information) as a catalyst for current metropolitan transformations. Therefore, this concept describes the result of the "spontaneous" process of clumping different uses in some specific fragments of the metropolitan tissue, which can be considered "places of centrality" (De las Rivas and Paris, 2014).

Territorial nodes are aggregations of functions located at those crossroads in which infrastructures connect different flows (Portas, Domingues and Cabral, 2011). They are spaces where the modal exchange takes place, and concepts of "proximity" and "distance" rely on connections to networks more than on geometrical positions. The variety of possible combinations is heterogeneous, both in terms of functions and networks/nodes, and their location. Thus, the concept of "node" is unstable (Amin and Thrift, 2002).

Unlike in consolidated urban hierarchies, current nodes don't show specific diagrams of spatial connection and their role is malleable. They assume the role of interchange and transmission hubs (Castells, 1989). The more flows and spokes converge on them, the larger and deeper their territorial influence. Therefore, the geography of the accessibility to physical infrastructures and digital flows is a key element to differentiate nodes and their territorial relevance. Also when they are not public, they can become a sort of local commons, which take on a role of provider of shared spaces for their specific contexts. At the same time, they contribute to "polarization" processes of metropolitan spaces, influencing existing territorialities. An attempt to define and design roles, features and potentialities of contemporary metropolitan hotspots is proposed through the conceptualization of Urban Digital Nodes within the context of the "smart region" between Milan and Turin (Morandi, Rolando and Di Vita, 2016).

More than fragments: drivers of urban/regional change

According to the described conceptual framework, a new layer of places/ nodes with different identities integrates – and sometime conflicts – with existing cities and consolidated urban patterns. Spaces that exist as something more than enclosures can be found in a rich set of different situations where, sometimes, they assume the role of centralities at different scales. The hypothesis is that they could act as drivers of innovation in relation to different conditions and localizations of metropolitan patterns, involving existing contexts as well as introducing new functions, actors, opportunities – along with new risks – within consolidated fabrics.

In Southern Milan, several examples convey the rich complexity of nodes' systems through their different scales (from local/neighbourhood to metropolitan/regional one), aggregation degrees, development stages and different kinds of networks attracted by or connected to these spaces.

Assago/Milanofiori north district

This cluster of different activities is located in between two municipalities (Assago and Rozzano), 15 km from the city centre, but just next to the administrative border of Milan (Figure 1.6). The cluster, formerly developed around a major road link, has been recently connected to the public transport network by means of the extension of an underground line. Assago/Milanofiori maintains a peculiar identity and holds a specific role at the edge of Southern Milan, primarily due to the size of the aggregation, the richness and complexity of the involved activities and their level of integration as well as the amount of liveliness, the multimodal accessibility, the attractiveness of the public space, and the quality of the urban, landscape, and architectural design. The settlement process started in the mid-seventies when a great amount of the agricultural area (150 hectares) were transformed to host a business district. The municipality of Milan had decided not to provide zones for tertiary function in the general town plan *(Piano Regolatore Generale)*, which created a bubble of investors searching for cheap headquarters in well-connected locations and equipped with parking spaces. Taking advantage of its accessibility, due to a crossroad of two important infrastructures of private mobility (i.e., the urban trace of the motorway A7 Milan-Genoa and the A50, ring road of the city), the district grew in different phases, progressively including offices, a congress hall, a 500 bed hotel, sport facilities, and a shopping mall of 12,000 sqm GLA. A large concert hall was built, and later the *"Teatro della luna"* and the shopping mall doubled in size. A new retail park is located in the northern part of the sector, together with offices and housing blocks, several activities such as the UCI multiplex, the Virgin gym, the Hotel, a food court, and several services integrating the existing facilities. Some elements seem to represent a step forward in the realization of a new, multifunctional pole, not just for the Rozzano municipality, nor for the city of Milan, but within the broader regional context (Morandi and Paris, 2013).

The place is a node where flows of consumers and goods converge, and where people produce and share information due to the concentration of services and leisure activities offered, related mainly with shopping, sport, and culture. The last expansion phase, from 2006 up to the present, reveals an interesting change in the developers' strategy, which involved different branded architectural firms in the development of a new masterplan. This attempt, aimed at coordinating the interventions and creating a specific identity for this place also represents a different approach to the implementation of retail platforms in the outskirts of Milan, some of them caught in a process of shrinkage and lack of perspective of economic success, despite new openings of very large and over-branded shopping centres. Integrating functions in a node quite accessible from both the city and the region in a varied pattern of metropolitan landscapes could contribute to the process of polycentric reorganization at the regional scale, through the improvement of the physical and social relationships within the southern sector of the city. This character relies on the quality of the design of some of its transitional/public spaces (i.e., the public square, some public service, etc.) that became a sort of shared space for the inhabitants.[5] The connection with public transport and, finally, the increasing urban/metropolitan urbanity (i.e., alternative, but integrated with the traditional urbanity of central spaces) have also played central roles in this transformation.

Fondazione Prada

The Milan venue of the Fondazione Prada (Figure 1.8) is a 28,340 sqm compound of ten buildings, close to the Porta Romana railway and Lodi TIBB subway stations, comprised of an art gallery devoted to showing the Prada contemporary art collection and to organize temporary exhibitions. It hosts a theatre, bar, offices, and a library located in a former distillery. Opened in 2015 (architectural design by OMA), the spatial distribution of this campus is marked by a shared ground floor open to the visitors. This urban element, together with a new skyscraper along with a gold painted tower, have become a landmark for the neighbourhood and, more in general, for this sector of the city.

The setting up of Fondazione Prada follows one of the current trends for luxury stakeholders who integrate art and design in their fields of action to diversify their investments and, at the same time, to promote their brand. These operations create local hubs of stakeholders and communities' networks related to the contemporary art market, cosmopolitan luxury customers (e.g., tourists, business travellers, and wealthy people). Yet, these constructs also attract those who have come to be referred to as part of the larger "creative class".[6] At the same time, within these kinds of initiatives, international stakeholders and developers often involve local contexts and identity as key elements of their commercial, but also cultural proposal, using these qualities to promote their products and brands on global markets (Paris and Fang, 2017). In this specific case, the Fondazione represents the materialization of an open structure where artists, architects, and designers exchange knowledge, but also share time and space, in a location well connected and close to the city centre, but often neglected by important art events and mainstream exhibitions. The gallery works together with several renting spaces where new designers and creatives can display their products and/or organize events. Together with the library, the education program tries to explore new ways for sharing knowledge and communicating art, also for children. Bringing different recipients together and introducing a set of events (performances, permanent and temporary exhibitions, annual festivals, and special happenings for specific recurrences like design week or fashion week) the Fondazione Prada became a new cultural venue for Milan and for a much larger context

In addition, Prada serves as a node of immaterial networks, such as for similar institutions which are developing as tools to drive investments in cultural activities, also as an opportunity for fiscal advantages, but with and simultaneously taking on a significant role as urban developers, such as the new Fondazione Feltrinelli headquarters in Milan.[7]

The "smart triangle" and Open Dot in the Porta Romana-Vettabbia district

A program of digital infrastructure has been recently fostered by the local government within a partnership of mixed actors,[8] funded by the EU Horizon 2020 program.[9] The Sharing Cities Project aims at developing "demonstration districts in 'lighthouse' cities like Lisbon, London and Milan which will implement replicable urban digital solutions and collaborative models. The Royal Borough of Greenwich in London, Porta Romana-Vettabbia in Milan (Figure 1.8), and downtown Lisbon will retrofit buildings, introduce shared electric mobility services, and install energy management systems, smart lamp posts and an urban sharing platform through engaging with citizens".[10]

The Milan district has been selected due to the presence of both decline and dynamic conditions and for the opportunity to connect the fringe between urban and agricultural land.[11] Different layers are forecasted to implement the project, dealing with technological and social innovation. The presence of several associations in the third sector field is also considered an important asset for the project, together with the reuse of semi-abandoned sites, such as former *cascine*. Another action is the Smart City Lab for the realization of a start-up incubator in via Ripamonti. The City Lab is a new typology of facility supported by the state and the local government to foster digital innovation in new manufacturing. Therefore, the interest for the inclusion of the "smart triangle" among the knowledge-based nodes, depends on its intermediate scale, in between the city and the region.

Just outside the smart triangle, but close to the Porta Romana district, Open Dot is a small size makerspace and FabLab; a node of an important international knowledge-based network. It was founded in 2014 as a spin-off of Dot Dot Dot, a multidisciplinary architecture, design, and prototypes production firm. Also in this case, the activity is located inside an aggregate of former industrial buildings, under transformation first through the action of artisans and currently increasingly oriented to host "creative workers". Open Dot presents itself as an exchange and meeting point, dedicated to experimentation, innovation and research. The set of activities developed in Open Dot is a paradigm of digital fabrication places, addressed towards education at quite different levels: the neighbourhood schools on one side and, on the other side, a node of the international network of the Fab Academy, the online training activity directly run by the MIT founder group of the makers' movement (Anderson, 2012; Gershenfeld, 2007).

A molecular pattern of different forms of centralities

It is possible to take Southern Milan as a testing ground due to its specific situation, where nodes, the urban realm and a remaining rural landscape maintain their own identities. This chapter collects a sample of those nodes in which the relation with physical (i.e., public and private transport, logistic, open spaces) and immaterial networks (i.e., information and data, communities of interests, and/or people), and the presence of knowledge-based functions (i.e., specialized services, culture, education, creative productions, etc.) represent a territorial asset, which increases the attractiveness, for users and customers, of those spaces and the competitive advantages for investors and stakeholders, but also for public actors (Porter, 1989). Due to their complexity, these nodes are also spaces of production and consumption of goods, services, information, and experiences and, according to their specific offer, represent a materialization of the experience economy (Pine and Gilmore, 2011).

As pointed out by Pancholi, Yigitcanalar and Guaralda (2015), these spaces provide examples showing the result of the inter-action of global knowledge-based networks and local realities (Asheim, 2007; Inkinen, 2015). Often, they become a driver for innovative forms of consumption, co-produced by firms and customers (Pi-Feng and Chung-Shing, 2012) influencing the living practices of users and, therefore, the spaces in which they take place. By that way, they involve opportunities and risks of segregation (of spaces), exclusions (of users), and over-specialization of functions related with the physical, socio-economic, and symbolic role of nodes within the urban context. In this sense, the specific condition of Southern

Milan represents a catalyst and not only a context for the development of these knowledge based nodes.

The Assago/Milanofiori node (Figure 1.6) rose up as a "banal" operation aimed at maximizing real estate revenues related to the colonization of a well-located rural area. Within this transformation, the relevance of the role played by the private actors unfolds the weakness of public actors and the lack of a strategy for the localization of retail poles leaded by a supra-local body. This is a "consumption-based" (Pavitt, 1984) node, marked by the attractive power of functions and users and the high accessibility due to mobility infrastructures. Knowledge here refers to the consumption experience and to data produced and shared – offline and online – by the customers and other actors involved. Therefore, recent insertions of new public/shared spaces, the arrival of public transport and the density of involved functions provide the development with spontaneous uses of the physical space by its inhabitants. Moreover, it represents a peculiar form of centrality, a "different place" within a humdrum urban/rural space and contributing to the configuration of the current multipolar pattern of the Milan urban region.

The Fondazione Prada (Figure 1.8) venue is a pioneering intervention, where a "lucid" – and wealthy – actor developed an outstanding project, demonstrating that the involvement of an archistar, the attractiveness of contemporary art, and brilliant branding are enough to generate attention for previously anonymous locations within an urban region, also thanks to immaterial networks for a global audience. The marketing campaign based on creativeness and soft power seems to point out a potential future development of the area that must be sustained through an original offer of spaces and activities. Otherwise, all this narrative risks becomes merely an empty mystification and a tool for the exploitation of private capital without any creation of urban value or generation of fertile exchanges between the city and this "isle".

The area of the "smart triangle", in the Porta Romana-Vettabbia district (Figure 1.8) collects a set of transformations and represents an incremental process based on pilot experiences. This case study points out the relevance of the sharing approach as a link between different projects and aspects of these interventions. Within this sort of living lab, developers should produce original knowledge and the system relies on bottom-up actions as well as social and technologic innovations. In this case, the public actor deserves a strong protagonist role, due to its position as a key financial and strategic player. In parallel, the experience of Open Dot represents a different, if not alternative, example of grafting new forms of production on a solid and diffuse knowledge base related to design and manufacturing.

Conclusions

The excursus on Southern Milan shows that the consolidated, but updated, figure of networks and nodes remains a fertile operative tool, able to explain some current territorial patterns, although influenced by ongoing processes. Therefore, nodes show an evolution that combines current socio-economic trends and a change in conditions that influenced their formation (reduction of public investments in infrastructures, restrictions for soil-consumption, interest of private actors for more urban locations, growing relevance of knowledge economy and immaterial networks). These transformations play a role within the future metropolitan scenario of Milan. If they act as catalyst, they should produce a spill-over effect, creating a network of places and territories. At the same time, if they maintain their current identity as enclaves disconnected from the contexts where they are located, the risk is that networks, instead of connecting, become a sort of border or limit for their multifaceted flows.

Notes

1 IFOM is a cancer research institute partner of cutting-edge scientific organizations located in India and Singapore.
2 The European Institute of Oncology (*IEO*) is a centre for excellence in cancer prevention, early diagnosis and effective treatment.
3 This greyfield is one of the larger development areas included in the 2012 Milan urban plan.
4 For instance, tertiary functions (as headquarters of Bottega Veneta, and the Italian venues of LVMH, Motorola and McGraw-Hill), leisure (as the glamour club Plastic Palace) and mixed-use containers (as the co-working and makerspace Talent Garden Calabiana, or the fashion event space Fabbrica Orobia 15).
5 Within the new masterplan, among other tertiary functions there are two housing projects and this hybrid compound represent an innovative experiment for the Milanese context, normally marked, out of the urban dense tissues, by the presence of mono-functional retail aggregates and some superplaces (Morandi and Paris, 2015) but where the inhabitants are only temporary and the housing function is excluded.
6 See Chapter 4.
7 See Chapter 8.
8 Partnership: public and private companies in the field of sustainable energy provision and mobility, Politecnico di Milano, Legambiente
9 *Horizon 2020, call* 'Smart Cities and Communities solutions integrating energy, transport, ICT sectors through lighthouse projects'
10 www.sharingcities.eu/
11 In the same sector, another project has just been approved and granted by the European Commision: "Open Agri" involves a partnership of actors, some of them active in the field of research and education, led by the Milan Municipality.

References

Amin, A. and Thrift, N. (2002). *Cities: Reimagining the urban.* Cambridge: Polity Press.

Anderson, C. (2012). *Makers: The new industrial revolution.* London: Random House Penguin.

Ascher, F. (1995). *Métapolis ou l'avenir des villes.* Paris: Odile Jacob.

Asheim, B. (2007). Differentiated knowledge bases and varieties of regional innovation systems. *Innovation: The European Journal of Social Science Research,* 20(3), pp. 223–241.

Castells, M. (1989). *The informational city: Information technology, economic restructuring, and the urban-regional process.* Oxford: Basil Blackwell.

De las Rivas, J.L. and Paris, M. (2013). Valladolid come punto d'incontro di paesaggi: dalle letture a scala intermedia alla pianificazione del territorio. *Monograph. Research,* 5, pp. 84–87.

De las Rivas, J.L. and Paris, M. (2014). Strengthening the territorial position of Valladolid through planning strategies: Networks, patterns, centralities. *Journal of Civil Engineering and Architecture,* 9, pp. 1168/1177.

Fishman, R. (1987). *Bourgeois utopias: The rise and fall of suburbia.* New York: Basic Books.

Font, A. (2007). *La explosión de la ciudad.* Madrid: Ministerio de Vivienda.

Garreau, J. (1992). *Edge city: Life on the new frontier.* New York: Anchor Books.

Genette, G. (1992). *Esthétique et poétique.* Paris: Seuil.

Gershenfeld, N. (2007). *Fab: The coming revolution on your desktop-from personal computers to personal fabrication.* New York: Basic Books.

Inkinen, T. (2015). Reflections on the innovative city: Examining three innovative locations in a knowledge bases framework. *Journal of Open Innovation: Technology, Market, and Complexity,* 1(8), pp. 1–23.

Knox, P.L. (2008). *Metroburbia.* Piscataway: Rutgers University Press.

Morandi, C. and Paris, M. (2013). From retail polarities to superplaces: New tools to undesrtand recent transformations in retail geography in Italy: the Assago (MI) case. *AE – Architecture & Education Journal,* 8–9, pp. 427–448.

Morandi, C. and Paris, M. (2015). A territorial role for superplaces?/Quale ruolo nel territorio per i superluoghi? *Archivio di Studi Urbani e Regionali,* 112, pp. 101–126.

Morandi, C., Rolando, A. and Di Vita, S. (2016). *From smart city to smart region, digital services for an internet of places.* Cham: Springer.

Pancholi, S., Yigitcanalar, T. and Guaralda, M. (2015). Public space design of knowledge and innovation spaces: Learnings from Kelvin Grove Urban Village, Brisbane. *Journal of Open Innovation: Technology, Market and Complexity,* 1(1), pp. 1–13.

Paris, M. and Fang Li. (2017). From luxury to prestigious place-making: an overview. In: M. Paris, ed., *Making prestigious places: How luxury influences the transformation of cities.* London: Routledge, pp. 1–20.

Pavia, R. (2002). *Babele: la citta` della dispersione.* Roma: Meltemi.

Pavitt, K. (1984). Sectoral patterns of technical change: towards a taxonomy and a theory', *Research Policy*, 13, pp. 343–373.

Pi-Feng, H. and Chung-Shing, L. (2012). A note on value creation in consumption-oriented regional service clusters. *Competitiveness Review*, 22(2), pp. 170–180.

Pine, J.B. and Gilmore, J.H. (2011). *The experience economy*. Cambridge: Harvard Business.

Portas, N., Domingues, A. and Cabral, J. (2011). *Políticas urbanas II: Transformações, regulação e projectos*. Lisboa: Fundação Calouste Gulbenkian.

Porter, M.E. (1989). *The competitive advantage of nations*. New York: Free Press.

Secchi, B. (1994). Figure del rinnovo urbano. *Casabella*, 614, pp. 16–17.

Soja, E.W. (2011a). Regional urbanization and the end of the metropolis era. In: G. Bridge and S. Watson, eds., *The new Blackwell companion to the city*. Malden: Wiley-Blackwell, pp. 679–689.

Soja, E.W. (2011b). Beyond postmetropolis. *Urban Geography*, 32, pp. 451–469.

7 Urban change and geographies of production in North-East Milan

Simonetta Armondi

Introduction

This contribution challenges – as does the book as a whole – a unified and closed conceptualization of Milan meant as Milan municipality, a set and limited jurisdictional level. This chapter will help to highlight the growing integration processes and contentious territorialities that renovate the transscalar relationship between the Milan urban region and Milan municipal area (Figures 1.2–1.7). The socio-spatial effects of urbanization don't just weaken with distance from the centre to some outer boundary. This multiscalar spread of regional urbanization is almost impossible to recognize in a conventional metropolitan perspective (Soja, 2011).

North-East Milan is a particularly complex spatial context, one of the former heartlands of Western European Fordism, which experienced a significant level of de-industrialization and a reconfiguration of production at the local scale, with the crisis of the Fordist mass production system. In the 1990s, North-East Milan was also subject to an intensive process of tertiarization, triggered by decline in the manufacturing sector and exacerbating some of the structural change processes already initiated in previous years. With a densely populated and infrastructured territory (Figures 1.5–1.6), North-East Milan is currently facing a second round of economic restructuring following the economic shock caused by the global financial crisis in 2008.

This chapter reflects the change of an established sector of the urban region to grasp the socio-spatial relation and dynamics that characterized the geography of North-East Milan during three main phases of capitalist development:

- the long phase of growth and urban expansion;
- the season of the Fordist crisis and the subsequent economic restructuring;

• the current cycle of economic and spatial shrinkage after the 2008 global crisis.

This chapter analyses the different construction processes and treatment of problems that define the space of public policies and private transformation projects. In the public debate North-East Milan is usually defined as North Milan, and we follow this convention.

Subsequent rounds of spatial restructuring in the North Milan urban region

For much of the last century, North Milan in general, and Sesto San Giovanni in particular, represented a kind of incarnation – the purest – of the Fordist model of development in which the crisis of that industrial geography assumed dramatic proportions and visibility. North Milan as an historic region of the economic development of Milan and Lombardy, can be interpreted as an enlightening "litmus test", emblematic of the current processes.

In the recent strategic plan of the Metropolitan City of Milan (2016), North Milan is identified with seven municipalities (Cinisello Balsamo, Cormano, Bresso, Cologno Monzese, Sesto San Giovanni, Cusano Milanino, and Paderno Dugnano), in an area of 5,788 hectares with important demographic weight – registering 315,494 inhabitants – and intense economic activities with 120,039 employees. However, the boundaries of North Milan do not exist from the administrative point of view. The geography of North Milan as a whole is a policy outcome and was structured in the early twentieth century through a variety of investment decisions and policy agendas imposed from outside and other scales – industrial decentralization – and by reason of local social processes, for instance the formation of a skilled labour force.

In addition, the northern urban strip of Milan municipality area has been home to the Pirelli industry from the early twentieth century. Industrial plants were abandoned in the 1980s, and after an international urban design competition, Bicocca Project was realized between 1983 and 2008. This is one of the largest urban transformation projects in Milan by size (700,000 square meters) with innovative urban functions in culture and knowledge economy such as: the new Milano-Bicocca university, the Pirelli Hangar Bicocca (Figure 1.8) – one of the largest centres of contemporary art in Europe – research centres, a residential neighbourhood, and the great Arcimboldi theatre (Figure 1.6).

Looking at the spatial pattern side, two elements generated the North Milan geography:

• the territorial structure formed along the northern axis, governed by an investment of the ruling class between the 1800s and the 1900s since the industrial settlements between the northern part of Milan and the municipality of Sesto San Giovanni (in relation to the railway line) and the location of several housing developments for the working class, concerning the municipality of Cinisello in the 1950s and Cologno Monzese in the 1960s.

•   The spontaneous process of metropolitan integration and the formation of large urban areas from east to west, from the Sempione area to the Vimercatese one, with a transverse link in the Milan urban region.

The trajectories of three municipalities are essential for the understanding of the nexus between production and spatial patterns.

The historical spatial transformation of Cinisello Balsamo and Cologno Monzese is linked to the large-scale heavy industry development of Sesto San Giovanni. Their growth as medium-size urban centres – with the ability to attract not only dormitory suburbs of social housing in Cinisello and self-construction housing in Cologno, as well as productive activities – occurred after the Second World War, much later than nearby Sesto San Giovanni. From 1951 to 1971 the population of Cinisello, for instance, increased from around 15,000 to more than 77,000. Cologno redefined its urban economic base following the model of the Mediaset system suppliers' network in the audiovisual sector.

The process of urbanization is one of the key elements within this broader geography of capitalist socio-spatial organization (Brenner, 2004). Sesto San Giovanni became the social and productive model of Fordist industry and labour organization. Establishments such as Breda, the Falck steel industry, and the Ercole and Magneti Marelli industry have long characterized the country's industrial ethos, marking a material and symbolic dimension embodying values and social practices closely linked to factory work and working class subscriptions to the Italian Communist Party. Consequently, the myth generated by these labour and industrial spatial patterns has labelled Sesto San Giovanni as, firstly, the Manchester and then, the Stalingrad of Italy.

Thus the crisis of the manufacturing industry in the steel and engineering sector (the last blast furnace was shut down in 1995) and the redefinition of the Fordist regulation system mainly hit Sesto San Giovanni – leaving many abandoned industrial buildings and areas – but it also ended up becoming the symbolic representation of the entire North Milan area. The demise of large industrial manufacturing plants was only one aspect of a more general process of transition of the overall production system, which involved both a deep-seated restructuring of the industrial manufacturing apparatus, and the emergence of new production patterns, also based on research and the application of new technologies related to the field of electronics, information technology and multimedia communication.

After the end of the Fordist/Keynesian cycle, North Milan exploited system-diversified production, with small and medium enterprises specialized in construction and trade and, on the manufacturing level, in engineering and in information and communication technologies.

Furthermore, North Milan's historically varied profile began to take on a unique role as "policymaker" and its borders became increasingly recognizable in the metropolitan area during the 1900s. The main processes of rescaling that built this territory up as a recognizable area and that led to the pioneering role of the North Milan area in local development policies were as follows.

First, on the national level, the recognition of the territory as a "crisis area" according to law 236/1993. Labelling North Milan as an industrial area in crisis within a national policy, not only had an influence on additional financial resources for the promotion of active employment policies and reindustrialization initiatives, but also a growing inter-relationship between the various municipalities in regards to redefining a development path for the area.

Second, on the local level, the establishment in 1996 of the North Milan Development Agency (ASNM), limited company under private law whose shareholders are the main four municipalities; the ASNM has gradually taken on the role of accompanying actor and pioneering promoter of local development, also supporting the drafting of a North Milan Strategic Plan.

Third, always on the local level, the practice of sharing policies between local governments and especially among "entrepreneurial" mayors directly elected by citizens by the mid-1990s.

Fourth, at that time on the national level, a different specific programming context – the so-called *programmazione negoziata* – started up in Italy. This type of negotiated programming had explicit contractual content which aimed to reconsider the tools and forms of public intervention in the economy, promoting endogenous economic development in weaker areas of the country (Governa and Salone, 2005).

Together, these processes and policies contributed to shaping North Milan; this territory is therefore the result of a plurality of processes, policies, framing, and reframing activities in which a number of different actors have participated on various levels.

After the decline of the Fordist model and the consequent dramatic deindustrialization, following the closure of large scale industry in the steel and metallurgical sectors, the production system had been severely weakened by the global financial crisis of 2008, with a 33 per cent decrease in employees in the manufacturing sector between 2001 and 2011 (Table 7.1).

The economy of North Milan has undergone a troublesome period. The shifting hierarchies of international economic networks passed it by for the most part, and even multinational companies like Oracle, but also headquarters and large electromechanical manufacturers such as Aab or Alstom

Table 7.1 North Milan before and during economic crisis: socio-economic data

	1971. Population	2011. Population	Tot. workers 2001	Tot. workers 2011	Change 2001–2011 workers (manufacturing)	Change 2001–2011 workers (commerce)	Change 2001–2011 workers (financial, insurance, real estate, professional and scientific sectors)	2011. Share of employees in innovative sector
Milan	1,732,000	1,242,123	688,427	773,571	-23%	5%	5%	0.18
North Milan[1]	324,977	304,601	102,015	108,064	-33%	8%	23%	0.91

Data source: PRIN Postmetropoli Atlas 2015.

industry, which set up business in the area in the early 2000s, partly left Sesto San Giovanni. This shift is partly counterbalanced by a high share of employees in innovative sector (Table 7.1).

Even the ASNM, after passing under the control of the province of Milan (its majority shareholder), which was subsequently renamed Milano Metropoli Spa, closed in 2013, leaving thirty employees out of work.

Mapping North Milan vacancies and spatial strategies

The next sections introduce four paradigmatic contexts in North Milan in which we analyse the nexus between the trans-scalar spatial issues and the redefinition of the urban economic basis in the current conjuncture.[2] The core of this analysis focuses on specific spatial projects and policies that spread throughout the North Milan urban region over the last three decades. Each section shows how new forms and scales of interventions have emerged since the 1990s, largely in response both to specific regulatory problems, and strategic vision issues.

2.1 The uncertain fate of the large vacant industrial area: former Falck and railway hub

The project of the former Falck steel industrial area in Sesto San Giovanni is a paradigmatic case of a large scale development project – the most important example of urban transformation and functional renewal – undertaken in the Milan urban region that traversed the three established periodizations of capitalist development.

There is a significant amount of vacant industrial areas in Sesto San Giovanni – around 235 hectares, about one fifth of its municipal area – suitable for potential transformation.

The entire area subject to intervention – 1,430,000 square meters – is the largest in the Milan urban region (Figure 1.6): larger even than that of Expo, which measures 1.1 million meters square.[3] Some authors sustain that this was the largest regeneration project of an industrial area in Europe.

Box 7.1   The former Falck area case

1980s–1995. Falck industrial activities suspended.

1995. First development project by Kenzo Tange commissioned by the Falck company. The project is focused around the realization of theme parks.

1997. First land use change in the Sesto land use plan (from industry to services, housing, and parks).

1998. International competition organized by ASNM on Falck areas urban park.

2000. Falck areas are sold to a local developer (Pasini) for about 190 million euro.

2001. Master plan for a business centre by a group directed by Mario Botta. The economic functions were strongly pushed forward by a private sector investment with a bank (Banca Intesa).

2001. Project proposal by Pasini for a residential project.

2004. New land use plan approved, reducing the volumes.

2005. Conflict between property owner and public administration. Pasini sells the areas to a national developer (Risanamento, owned by Zunino) for 218 million euro.

2006. First Master Plan proposal by Renzo Piano based on previous activities with working groups involving the citizens.

2007. Program Agreement between the Municipality and Lombardy region for the environment reclamation.

2009. New land use plan of the Sesto municipality.

2010. Risanamento files for bankruptcy. Risanamento sells the areas to a new developer, Sesto Immobiliare, then MilanoSesto, (405 million euro).

2011. New proposal based on a revision of Renzo Piano's Master Plan. Plan approved with 900,000 of park. Consequently Risanamento Spa is granted double the volumes given to the previous owner.

2012. Agreement Programming on the implementation of the City of Health and Research in the municipality of Sesto San Giovanni. The City gives the area to MilanoSesto, owner of Falck areas. Currently MilanoSesto holds the commission for the land reclamation (38 million euro). The Municipality will concede the area for free to the Lombardy Region, to build the City of Health and Research.

2016. Agreement between the developer and Fawaz Alhokair, a Saudi Arabian group. MilanoSesto sells 130,000 sqm (for 500 million euro) to Fawaz for the new development of a shopping centre and a leisure park.

The analysis of the complex and yet incomplete progress of the project (Box 7.1) does not confirm the existence of a pro-growth coalition.

Instead, we can find a deep-rooted left-wing municipality exhibiting a nostalgia for its industrial past and hesitance in defining a strong and shared trans-scalar policy agenda for urban renewal of the historical vacant industrial areas.

Early 2013 was a crucial time because with a trans-scalar governance process, regional and local governments and the private foundation (Besta neurological hospital and Milanese Tumor institute) signed their intention to join this project and agreed to search for practical solutions to the implementation thereof by relocalizing the two hospitals in a new City of Health and Research (180,000 square meters).

After twenty-one years of expectations, two competitions, the involvement of architects (Kenzo Tange, Mario Botta, Renzo Piano), and the recent new real estate investment by a Saudi Arabian global real estate investor-buyer, important issues like infrastructure and the high strategic trans-scalar potential of the advanced services localized in the activities of the City of Health and Research, but also to the development of the shopping centre and leisure park, were not outlined in the local, metropolitan, and regional settings of governance.

Temporary spatial re-appropriation in Mage

The recent crisis has resulted in a number of social, economic institutional experiments. One of them is related to temporary use of vacant spaces. Made in Mage, an incubator of fashion and sustainable design, is an experimental project of low-cost temporary reuse by the Temporiuso association, a professional network proposing to act as facilitator to local governments and with the support of university structures in low-budget projects of the temporary spatial reuse of vacant spaces. The goal is to promote and support craft and creative firms within the ambit of fashion and sustainable design who won the "Creativity Made in Mage" competition, assigning spaces for workshops and laboratories in free loan with fees management and start-up at the vacant General Stores of the Falck industry (Ma.Ge), part of the Sesto San Giovanni heritage of industrial archaeology.

From December 2010 to July 2013, Made in Mage encouraged the temporary re-use of buildings and empty or underused spaces by activating a start-up project of production activities related to the sectors of crafts, fashion, and sustainable design.

Without suggesting that the temporary use is integrally undesirable, a number of scholars have emphasized that temporary use initiatives promote the urban change in a way that, while on the one hand seems unusual, on the other hand passively contributes in a process of capitalist accumulation.

A new planning disaster in the former Magneti Marelli and Adriano neighbourhood

In Italy, as in other Southern European countries (Knieling and Othen-grafen, 2016), the financial industry has been strongly focused on housing business as a strategy for growth. The financial crisis and the subsequent economic downturn have had a widespread impact on the stagnation of the real estate property market and the contraction of the building sector.[4] The case of Adriano neighbourhood witnesses the end of that period of constant boom in the construction sector, and also underlines, once again, a lack of vision for reflecting an urban and regional future related to vacant spaces.

The area is part of the municipality of Milan, located near to the former Ercole Marelli industrial area (Figure 1.6), the former San Giuseppe farm, and adjacent to the municipal boundary of Sesto San Giovanni and is one of the several unfinished urban transformation projects in Milan.

The area is subject to two Integrated Intervention Programs within the planning documents of Milan. Approved in 2004, the two programs concern the 305,000 square meters industrial area, including the premises of the former Magneti Marelli industrial area, and a 170,000 square meters area for public use. Overall, the provisions contained in the two intervention programs outlined a single plan development project for the former Magneti Marelli and areas of San Giuseppe, a design involving the construction of public and private residential settlements and commercial and office areas around a large central park.

Twelve years on, only a few residential buildings have been completed, there is no public transport to the new Adriano neighbourhood, and buildings have been left unfinished. Consequently, the municipality of Milan is asking for ten million euro because two (now bankrupt) construction industry enterprises in the neighbourhood were forced to compensate the right to construct housing with works of public interest. After the failure in the private operating sector that required implementation of the "Adriano Marelli and San Giuseppe farm" Integrated Intervention Program, the Municipality used its power of proxy to finish part of the uncompleted works to the tune of 10,850,000 euro.

Thanks to the municipal resources, urbanization works – new piazzas and a park of 39,000 square meters – were already completed and the derelict San Giuseppe Farm structure was demolished.

This process, emblematic of the difficulty experienced by Italian real estate developers and the construction industry under the impact of the economic crisis, also uncovers the incapacity to create an integrated trans-scalar development project involving both Milan, and Sesto San Giovanni municipalities.

Re-imagining a different future in Cinisello Balsamo

In Italy, Cinisello Balsamo embodies one of the pioneering fields of local public innovations. Starting in the 1990s, a number of experimental projects have been started up with new opportunities offered by the European and national programming. Through partnership with private and community-based organizations, the municipal government has mobilized a range of cultural economy-led policies and infrastructure projects intended to promote urban change. A significant sample of policies and projects of urban transformations carried out by the Cinisello Balsamo municipality in order to distance itself from its historic "dormitory town" stigma, are the followings.

*   The city centre regeneration project, with the redevelopment of Piazza Gramsci (2003) designed by Dominique Perrault.
*   An international cultural project for the Milanese urban region: museum of contemporary photography (2004) in Villa Ghirlanda. It is the first public museum of photography in Italy.
*   Localization of cultural functions in the "Il Pertini" cultural centre, with library, auditorium, and café (2012).
*   New crucial elements of the metropolitan public transport: the new Milan-Cinisello Balsamo tramway (2008), and the inter-institutional program agreement (2016) related to the ongoing "Intermodal Hub Northern Milan", with an extension of subway line 5. The interchange of the subway and local public transport will also be integrated with a system of services for cyclists.
*   A new co-working space (2016) financed by a public bid for tenders attended by the municipality in partnership with other local associations. Cinisello Balsamo will soon have a space dedicated to co-working and start-up firms at Villa Forno, with a branch of the University of Milan-Bicocca and a digital library. The purpose of the project is to provide areas for self-employment and entrepreneurial activities, shared business space and support to young creative talents in starting up business. There is a potential link between this public policy and the agglomeration of new manufacturing, co-working, and 2.0 craftsmanship both in Sesto San Giovanni with the Co+Fabb private centre (3,400 square meters) and along Viale Monza in Milan[5] (Figure 1.8).
*   The Bicocca District for innovation and creativity (2016), a formal agreement between the local governments (Milan, Cinisello, Sesto) and the University of Milano Bicocca, Pirelli Foundation, Arcimboldi Theater, Siemens corporation, and Deutsche Bank, to link and promote education, training, research, culture, and entrepreneurship initiatives at the urban region scale.

Taken together these general processes and policy clusters shape a tendency to generate change through a new urban imagery.

Conclusion

To conclude, the current global socio-economic crisis is related to multiple local events of preceding cycles under capitalism and is manifested in a series of socio-spatial effects. It is in the present conjuncture, as it was in the 1960s and in the late 1990s, North Milan a territory of urban change, experimentation of new relationships between spatial organization, settlement forms of the new economies, and urban development that challenge both the traditional radiocentric urban image and the city/hinterland nexus? How do crisis and austerity shape urban regional geographies? The chapter has shown that in a time of austerity North Milan is witnessing the emergence of a much greater unevenness in local systems that has led to the development of a mosaic of differentiated productions of space.

In North Milan a number of controversial, entrenched spatial strategies emerge. We distinguish two distinctive lenses to analyse public policies and strategies that mobilize – both implicitly and explicitly – space and time as productive forces through various forms of investments and regulation.

– Singularity vs. multiplicity

Since the 2008 economic crisis, large scale development projects haven't captured the most interesting spatial transformations. On the one hand, the effects of the global crisis are making it difficult to carry out large urban transformation projects, such as in the Magneti Marelli and Falck areas. Some of those that are related to vast industrial vacant areas often stagnate due to the difficulties and bankruptcy of real estate investors and construction industry developers. There is little chance of investment, especially when compared to the demand of very large complex developments projects.

On the other hand, the singular large urban transformation project (former Falck and Magneti Marelli) has trans-scalar effects not only redesigning and "eradicating" the local geography of governance, but also getting stuck in a trans-scalar territorial relations system which was profoundly changed as a result of the economic recession. Nonetheless, large scale development projects are poorly integrated into the wider urban region processes and planning system. As a consequence, their impact on the urban area as a whole and on the areas where the projects are located remains ambiguous. Place branding in former Falck areas is a crucial example. The label "City of Health and Research" focuses on the representation of a healthy space, considered as a permanent, singular, and sanitized image of place, which nonetheless inevitably means highlighting some elements and neglecting others. Furthermore, the geopolitical domain of transregional policies and governance is remarkably absent. Although situated in the heart of the Lombardy region, former Falck areas (and the Magneti Marelli project) do not serve as a "model" for border-crossing initiatives and new networks. Despite representing the broadest example of former industrial area redevelopment projects, the former Falck areas do not even have strategic priority in national, regional, and metropolitan policies.

North Milan is also changing in a less visible and more incremental direction, through an array of micro-scale development projects. Nowadays, only in regards to Cinisello Balsamo local authority a sort of niche innovations can be identified. Local policies manage economic and social pressures, such as industrial crises and high unemployment rates, by introducing a multiplicity of changes and innovating the image of the city through a transscalar molecular projects and involving different actors.

– *Temporary vs. permanent*

The vast areas of numerous, small, old, and new ruins were scattered in many territories of North Milan as they were in other European and North American countries following the decline of the Fordist industry, but the 2008 global financial crisis also played its part. At the same time, suspended development projects have been implicated in financial and real estate speculation (former Falck, Magneti Marelli). In response, a range of different entities have attempted to lay claim to vacant spaces, also in terms of temporary reuse (Made in Mage).

Subsequent policies have promoted the recycling of vacant spaces back into the circuit of property development and financial speculation, or reuse thereof to create the spatial conditions for alternative types of urbanity. Considered thus, vacant space plays a key role in determining how cities will respond to both urban problems and wider global challenges.

According to Ferreri (2015) the temporary reuse of vacant spaces is a "tempting simplified narrative in which symptoms are confused with causes, and solutions are offered through purely administrative, or managerial actions" (Ferreri, 2015, p. 185), instead of focusing on the motives of austerity urbanism with the scarcity of available low-budget spaces for non-commercial uses and the socioeconomic conditions that trigger urban vacancies.

Consequently, the risk is that this temporariness could become an increasingly permanent trend in the framework of two seemingly separate itineraries related to vacancy: one for urban space as fixed, and this is the trajectory

108 *Simonetta Armondi*

for large scale real estate development projects for – sometimes outdated – mainstream functions, and the other for micro-scale spaces and temporary re-appropriation to which precarious creative and knowledge workers and social entrepreneurs are relegated.

Furthermore, urban development projects embody a series of processes that are associated with changing spatial scales of governance; these changes, in turn, reflect a shifting permanent or temporary geometry of power in the governing of urbanization. Across the geopolitics of global real estate the new phenomenon of real estate investments by foreign investor-buyers – such as in the former Falck areas – is emerging (Büdenbender and Golubchikov, 2017), inviting us to examine the structural capitalist forces that are central to contemporary urban political economies and thereby facilitate the temporary flow of foreign capital.

Notes

1 The data for North Milan are calculated as the sum of all data covering Cinisello Balsamo, Sesto San Giovanni, Cusano Milanino, Cormano, Bresso Cologno Monzese, and Paderno Dugnano.
2 For a general overview of the nexus between economic crisis and Italian territorial shrinkage see Armondi (2013).
3 See Chapter 8.
4 See Chapter 10.
5 The Milan City Council has developed a policy package aiming at support on one hand, co-working and makerspaces (see Chapter 5), and on the other hand, the nexus between workplaces and social innovation in "peripheral neighbourhoods" (Armondi and Bruzzese, 2017).

References

Armondi, S. (2013). What we talk about when we talk about productive territories: The case of shrinking Italy. *The International Journal of Architectonic, Spatial, and Environmental Design*, 6(3), pp. 62–76.
Armondi, S. and Bruzzese, A. (2017). Contemporary production and urban change: The case of Milan. *Journal of Urban Technology*.
Brenner, N. (2004). *New state space: Urban governance and the rescaling of the statehood*. Oxford: Oxford University Press.
Büdenbender, M. and Golubchikov, O. (2017). The geopolitics of real estate: Performing state power via property markets? *International Journal of Housing Policy*, 17(1), pp. 75–96.
Ferreri, M. (2015). The seduction of temporary urbanism. *Ephemera*, 15(1), pp. 181–191.

Governa, F. and Salone, C. (2005). Italy and European spatial policies: Polycentrism, urban network and local innovation practices. *European Planning Studies*, 13(2), pp. 265–283.

Knieling, J. and Othengrafen, F. eds. (2016). *Cities in crisis*. Abingdon: Routledge.

Soja, E.D. (2011). Regional urbanization and the end of metropolitan Era. In: G. Bridge and S. Watson, eds., *The new Blackwell companion to the city*. Hoboken: Wiley-Blackwell, pp. 679–689.

8 Urban change and innovation of functions and productions in the north-western transect of the Milan urban region

Stefano Di Vita

Introduction

In European cities, the local effects of the world crisis, not to mention the urban resilience to the economic downturn, differ. On the one hand, there is the deletion, rescaling, or slowing-down of large urban transformation projects, which have often remained incomplete (Knieling and Othengrafen, 2016). On the other, there is a spontaneous spread of molecular recycling interventions, which contributes to wider processes of spatial and socio-economic regeneration (Guallart, 2012). The Milan urban region's sector along the historical north-west radial axis is representative of these contrasting phenomena, as well as of twofold and opposing trends of the entire urban region[1]:

- a material and symbolic recentralization towards the urban core, where high value productions of services and goods have been growing;
- contrarily, an expansive trend towards the most external areas, where traditional but low value productions are still important.

Accordingly, this chapter aims at reflecting on the current dynamics along the north-western transect of the Milan urban region, which are strengthening its role within the ongoing spatial and socio-economic metamorphosis expressed by the development of hybrid places, functions, and productions, even though the negative effects determined by the chronical lack of a broad and shared vision.

From the urban core perspective to that of the urban region: a new interpretation

The north-western transect of the Milan urban region is historically innervated by a system of parallel roads and railways, connecting the urban core to the so-called Simplon and Olona conurbation,[2] to leisure areas (i.e., the new Arese shopping centre "Il Centro", or the Ticino River regional park), to transport hubs (i.e., the Malpensa international airport) (Figure 1.3), up to other Italian large cities (such as Turin) or European countries (such as France and Switzerland) (Figures 1.1 and 1.2). Accordingly, it is the most international of the radial axes connecting Milan to its multi-scalar surroundings. This is a role that it will also play in the future, responding to the ongoing implementation of new infrastructures:

• the strengthening of the historical radial axis through the upgrading of existing roads, motorways, and railways (also improving the accessibility to the Malpensa international airport);
• the completion of a new road system, which bypasses the urban core by crossing the entire northern area of the urban region, from Varese (West) to Bergamo (East), as well as from Rho (West) to Monza (East);
• the development of European Corridors 5 and 24 (Figures 1.1 and 1.2).

These new connections integrate the radial axis, that originate from the Milan historical centre, with new transversal links, which sometimes exclude the Milan municipal area. Therefore, they suggest an observation of the north-western transect from the (new) point of view of the urban region, rather than from the traditionally radiocentric perspective.[3]

The north-western sector of the Milan urban region still registers a widespread industrialization – made up mainly of small and medium enterprises – together with an ongoing service sector metamorphosis and internationalization of larger production firms, as well as growing demographic phenomena of aging population, immigration, social polarization, and commuting, which are typical of the entire urban region. Differences can be recognized between the main city and its immediate surroundings (more attractive for information intensive functions and productions) and the outer areas (more attractive for supplier dominated enterprises) (Bolocan Goldstein, Botti and Pasqui, 2011). Despite a general trend of "poor metropolization" has also been affecting the north-western homogeneous areas of the Milan Metropolitan City (called "Nord Ovest"[4] and "Alto Milanese"[5]),[6] along the same axis other strong territorial economies can be identified within most external areas of the wider urban region: from the Varese agglomeration (public administration and mechanics), to the Malpensa agglomeration (aeronautics and logistics) (Figure 1.4) (Centro Studi PIM, 2016).

Within this context, the observed territorial transect reflects the dynamics of the Milan urban change process, both temporally and spatially. Regarding the temporal dimension, it shows the following transitions (Figures 1.6, 1.7 and 1.8):

• from historical compounds formed by big Fordist productive platforms (such as Alfa Romeo, with the 1906 factory in Milan Portello and the 1963 plant in Arese, closed in 1982 and 2005 respectively), to new polifunctional centralities. For instance, "Porta Nuova" (which took over some vacant spaces in front of the Milan Porta Garibaldi railway station), "CityLife" (under development in the historical Milan Trade Fair's exhibition venue) and the ongoing transformation of the former Alfa Romeo plant in Arese;

• from articulated manufacturing systems (such as in Milan Bovisa and Stephenson), to new creative districts (through the ongoing regeneration processes in Milan Isola-Porta Garibaldi-Porta Nuova and Bovisa-Dergano);

• from historical compounds formed by main university campuses of the city, to the (still in planning phase) innovative integration of universities and research centres with new manufacturing activities (such as in the former Milan Bovisa gasometers and in the Expo 2015 site between Milan and Rho).

Concerning the spatial dimension, it shows the city upgrade at the scale of the urban region, supporting an innovative interpretation of urban phenomena, for instance through (Figure 1.6 and 1.7):

• the spread of private company headquarters just outside the Milan historical centre (such as Unicredit, Coima, and Unipolsai in the "Porta Nuova" area, and Generali in the "CityLife" area), as well as of polifunctional centralities beyond the urban core (for instance, through the ongoing re-development of the former Alfa Romeo plant in Arese);

• the relocation of the Milan Trade Fair from the historical exhibition venue in the former "Piazza d'Armi", just outside the Milan historical centre (1923–2005), to the new one in suburban municipal areas of Rho and Pero (since 2005);

• the shift of the Expo site from the Porta Venezia public garden in the Milan historical centre (1881 National Expo), to the Simplon public garden and the former "Piazza d'Armi", just outside the city inner ringroad (1906 International Expo), up to abandoned greenfields between the municipal areas of Milan and Rho (2015 World Expo);

• the doubling of the Politecnico di Milano's technological campus (still not completed, but gradually opened since 1989) and the proposal to relocate the Università degli Studi di Milano's scientific campus from the historical Città Studi district, centrally placed, to the peripheral Bovisa brownfields and the suburban Expo 2015 site, respectively.

From the industrial development to a knowledge-based and creative economy: the strengthening of a broader city scale

The north-western transect of the Milan urban region corresponds to one of the most urbanized and industrialized areas in Northern Italy, generated by long-term processes of widespread urbanization and countryside industrialization in a variety of sectors (such as mechanics, electronics and mechatronics, chemical and pharmaceutical, metal, textile, and leather industries, often gathered in clusters) (Bolocan Goldstein, Botti and Pasqui, 2011). Despite its internal articulation, this area integrates the north-western neighbourhoods of the Milan municipality with a new city, called "Alto Milanese/Valle dell'Olonia" (Boeri, Lanzani and Marini, 1993) and formed by overlapping two different conurbations (Figures 1.2, 1.3, and 1.5):

• the historically dense Simplon and Olona conurbation, along the radial axis;
• the following fractal East-West conurbation, transversal to the radial axis, along the hills from Novara to Bergamo (Bolocan Goldstein, Botti and Pasqui, 2011).

The origins of this urban system can be traced back to the long history of the entire country, even though the process of urbanization was accelerated by the Milan industrial revolution after the Italian Unification in 1861. This economic and demographic take-off corresponded to the start of the manufacturing and residential development in north Milan, in both the main city and the outer area between the Simplon infrastructural corridor (to the West) and the Brianza (to the East[7]). Therefore, within the north-western sector of the Milan urban region, this growth involved:

• inside the urban core, the former rural area of Bovisa, which hosted large production compounds – starting with the Candiani chemical plant, since the 1880s[8] (Figure 1.6) – subsequently integrated by small manufacturing, craftsmanship, and logistics enterprises, as well as by the city gasometers (Erba, Molon and Morandi, 2000);
• outside the urban core, the Olona Valley between Varese and Milan,[9] which hosted several factories, originally mainly textile (Bolocan Goldstein, Botti and Pasqui, 2011) – such as the famous Bassetti in Rescaldina.

Within this process, former rural villages found themselves affected by a very disordered urban development, characterized by a frequent mix of industrial plants and worker houses, in a very dense and low-quality urban tissue. Whilst the first phase of this manufacturing and residential development was supported by new networks of railways and tramways, after the Second World War it was mostly sustained by growth in the motorway system.

In the urban core, the majority of factories were closed in the 1970s and 1980s because of their obsolescence and decreasing competitiveness. In the observed territorial transect, an example of relocalization is that of the Alfa Romeo car manufacturing plants. A first transfer was in the 1960s, when the historical Milan Portello plant moved to the new, bigger plant in Arese, within the Simplon and Olona conurbation, where it found and contemporarily generated a dynamic environment of supplier firms (Figure 1.6). According to a process of productive rationalization and reconfiguration – following the workers' protests of the 1960s, the car market crises of the 1970s and the introduction of environmental issues in the 1980s – a second transfer occurred in the 1990s, when Alfa Romeo closed its largest industrial plant in Arese, and relocated its car production to other factories of the Fiat group. The surviving supplier firms therefore needed to rebuild their business networks, and to extend them worldwide.

According to this de-industrialization trend, the current Milan urban change process started, dividing itself into different phases. A first pre-crisis phase was mainly directed at the real estate exploitation of industrial brownfields. Afterwards, the current post-crisis phase is also characterized by the development of new hybrid works and workplaces, meanwhile devoted to (material and immaterial) productions of advanced services and high quality goods in relation to the growth of a knowledge-based and creative economy (Mariotti, Pacchi and Di Vita, 2017).

This metamorphosis has articulated in both large urban transformation projects, and molecular but wider urban regeneration processes, thus contributing to spread new urban centralities and to renew entire neighbourhoods (Figures 1.6, 1.7, and 1.8). Among the main urban transformation projects promoted within the north-western sector of the urban region,[10] the most relevant are (Figure 1.6):

- the new "Maciachini Centre" business district in the former Carlo Erba factory area, as well as the new polifunctional centralities of "Porta Nuova" near the Porta Garibaldi railway station and "Portello Nord" in the former Alfa Romeo factory area, within the Milan municipality;
- the new polifunctional centralities in the former Alfa Romeo factory area between Arese and Lainate, and in the former Cantoni factory area in Legnano;

- the expansion of the Milan Trade Fair's exhibition venue in the "Portello Sud" brownfield and vacant spaces, within the Milan municipality, and the subsequent development of its new exhibition venue in the former Agip refinery area, between Rho and Pero;
- the new Expo 2015 exhibition site, located between Milan and Rho, near the new Milan Trade Fair's exhibition venue.

These interventions are joined by others, which are still under development within the Milan municipality, even though the crisis (in particular, that of the real estate market) has been affecting their completion and their implementation (which is often downgraded) has been going on slowly (Figure 1.6):

- the new polifunctional centralities of "CityLife" in the historic Milan Trade Fair's exhibition area and "Cascina Merlata" in a large vacant space at the edge of the main city;
- the reconfiguration of the former industrial Stephenson district to develop new productive and commercial activities.

Potential future transformations are, furthermore, expressed by the following long-term projects, though as yet they remain in the pipeline and their implementation is still uncertain (Figures 1.6 and 1.7):

- the reuse of the former Farini railyard and the renovation of the Ospedale Sacco, within the Milan municipality, together with the completion of the Bovisa brownfields' transformation (until now fragmentally implemented) through the development of a technological park, despite the recent downsizing of the university campus opened by the Politecnico di Milano since 1989;
- the completion of the former Alfa Romeo factory area's transformation between Arese and Lainate, in order to develop new productive activities;
- the post-event reuse of the Expo 2015 site, between Milan and Rho, according to the current proposals of the Human Technopole (promoted by the Italian Government), the Nexpo innovative firms' district (promoted by Assolombarda[11]), and a new university campus (promoted by the Università degli Studi di Milano), which have replaced the original plans of real estate exploitation;
- the reuse of the former Enel power plant in Castellanza, as well as of the former Italtel, Bull, and Agip factory areas in Settimo Milanese and Pregnana Milanese, also to house new productive activities.

The counterpart of these large urban transformation projects is represented by molecular but wider urban regeneration processes, particularly within the urban core. In the north-western sector of the Milan municipality, examples are the Isola-Porta Garibaldi-Porta Nuova district[12] (Figure 1.8) – including already-gentrified neighbourhoods (such as Brera, in the historical centre) and growing commercial ones (such as the Sarpi area, better known as Chinatown) – and former working-class neighbourhoods in the Bovisa-Dergano district.[13] Despite their specificities – concerning the main economic sectors of their new productive activities and the social profiles of their new residents – similarly, these districts have been attracting several new commercial activities, as well as new creative, cultural, digital, and media productions, often located in innovative and hybrid workplaces (Bruzzese and Tamini, 2014): for instance, the new Fondazione Feltrinelli cultural centre (Figure 1.8) – including the Microsoft House – the PoliHub incubator, and several co-working spaces and makerspaces. Unlike large urban transformation projects, this spatial and socio-economic regeneration process seems to be not penalized, but rather exploited by the long, far-reaching economic crisis of 2008, as its growth has increased particularly since 2010. It may represent a challenge for urban dynamics stimulated through a new post growth-dependent approach, so that even the recent Milan City Council policies have been supporting them (Mariotti, Pacchi and Di Vita, 2017).

Large urban transformation projects and single recycling interventions included in widespread urban regeneration processes have showed common features:

- their transcalarity, often being local nodes of wider cultural and socio-economic networks (from macro-regional to global);
- their connections with existing and new infrastructural corridors, which prove themselves as priority axes for metropolization phenomena.

Together with this articulated urban change process, the strengthening of large scale infrastructures – from the new terminal of Malpensa international airport (opened in 1998), to the new high-speed train line Milan-Turin (opened in 2006–2009) along the European Corridor Seville-Kiev (Figures 1.1 and 1.2) – has confirmed not only that the consolidated urban phenomena within the observed territorial transect can no longer be ignored, but also that its traditionally international perspective has been growing.

From monofunctional compounds and districts, to hybrid urban places, functions, and productions: challenges and potentials of a strategic project

The north-western sector of the Milan urban region clearly represents the urban change process which has led to the transformation and reuse of monofunctional compounds and districts of the industrial metropolis (such as productive platforms and systems, as well as university campuses, originally closed to surrounding neighbourhoods). Initially, this transformation and reuse mostly consisted of large polifunctional centralities, which were mainly oriented to a real estate development, even though they also contributed to promote a new city image and they often host important new functions, able to place Milan within world city networks (Taylor, 2004). Now, it is made up of both big projects and regeneration processes, also devoted to innovative and hybrid urban places, functions and productions. In spatial terms, this urban change process is divided into two parallel systems (Figure 1.6):

• the first one, in Milan, to the south of the Simplon axis, where the ongoing reconfiguration has almost been completed (through large urban projects as "CityLife", "Portello Sud", and "Portello Nord");
• the second one, from Milan to the Simplon and Olona conurbation, to the north of the Simplon axis, where several potentials are yet to be taken advantage of (within huge transformation areas as Farini railyards, Bovisa, Stephenson, Cascina Merlata, Expo 2015 site, and Arese).

There are several motives behind this slow implementation: the vast number of large areas involved, the governance complexity, the lack of a broad and shared vision, up to the recent real estate crisis. However, this system of big projects could be considered an opportunity to promote a new coordinated scenario, able to overcome their current fragmentation. A new strategic project for the entire north-western transect should extend from the centrality of "Porta Nuova" (Figure 1.6), just outside the Milan historical centre, to Malpensa international airport (Figure 1.3), in the outer part of the urban region (Bruzzese and Di Vita, 2016). According to local and international infrastructures, and to new urban places, functions, and productions devoted to a knowledge-based and creative economy, this project might lead to a new intermunicipal gateway city (Perulli, 2014), corresponding to the wider scale of urban phenomena determined by global processes of regional urbanization (Brenner, 2014).

Whilst both the "Documento Direttore del Progetto Passante" and the "Documento di Inquadramento Ricostruire la Grande Milano"[14] showed that the urban change process of the Milan municipal area should relate to its surroundings, beginning with its north-west axis, the projects observed in this chapter highlight common dynamics which cross the municipal borders. Within the wider context of the Milan urban region, that is difficult to (spatially and administratively) define into its post-metropolitan spatial configuration (Soja, 2011; Balducci, Fedeli and Curci, 2017), this could be a challenge, at least for both the future Metropolitan Territorial Plan and the annouced Strategic Agenda of the Milan Metropolitan City. These tools, which should follow the Metropolitan Strategic Plan,[15] could promote trans-scalar relations, not only with the local surroundings, but also with the wider urban region, and the macro-regional and global networks (Scott, 2001; Hall and Pain, 2006).

These relations could break physical and administrative barriers, as well as existing compounds made by former industrial plants (to re-develop), as well as historical university campuses or recent large urban transformation projects (frequently disconnected from their contexts).

This goal could be achieved through a trans-scalar approach, by improving the urban design quality of the project margins and by exploiting the potentials of new infrastructures (from the suburban railway system, to the high-speed train corridors).[16] This could be an opportunity to implement the Metropolitan Strategic Plan proposals for spatial and socio-economic regeneration, innovation, and inclusion (by improving not only economic attractiveness, but also spatial and environmental quality, and social cohesion[17]): on one hand, towards the development of the "Nord Ovest" homogeneous area as a hub of knowledge and innovation; on the other, towards the growth of the "Alto Milanese" homogeneous area by innovating its traditional manufacturing activities.

Considering the current lack of a broad and shared vision, most of the main players have been main urban entities such as "Fondazione Fiera Milano", Expo 2015, and Arexpo management companies, as well as local universities. However, their specific strategies have often related to their sectorial requirements, leading to frequent critical points. For instance (Figures 1.6 and 1.7):

•   the ongoing large transformation of the historical Milan Trade Fair's exhibition venue and the problematic Expo 2015 site's location within the Milan Trade Fair's areas close to its new exhibition venue between Rho and Pero, looking exclusively towards a real estate development;
•   the current parallel but independent strategies for the improvement of local universities, that risks economic unsustainability: on the one hand, the expansion of the Politecnico di Milano's new technological campus in the former Milan Bovisa gasometers and, on the other, the development of the Università degli Studi di Milano's new scientific campus in the Expo 2015 site, between Milan and Rho, without considering both their reciprocal spatial proximity and their indirect effects on the central Città Studi district, where they are historically located.

As Milan universities had already been some of the most important players in large transformation projects – from the new Università degli Studi di Milano Bicocca within the former Pirelli industrial plant,[18] to the new campuses of IULM and Università Bocconi in southern city districts[19] (Figure 1.7) (Balducci, Fedeli and Cognetti, 2010) – their role seems now to have changed. Both operations for the reuse of the Bovisa gasometers and the 2015 World's Fair area (Figure 1.6) – still in planning phase – seem more oriented to developing articulated nodes between trans-scalar networks of knowledge and innovation (public and private), rather than traditional real estate interventions (Briata, Di Vita and Pasqui, 2016). That is, nodes which interconnect universities, and public and private research centres (such as the Istituto Mario Negri in Bovisa and the future Human Technopole in the Expo 2015 site), with incubators and production firms aimed at developing innovative and hybrid services and manufacturing activities. An example is made up by the proposal for the location of the new IBM Watson Health centre[20] within the future Nexpo district, in the 2015 World's Fair area.

These two interventions seem to repropose the agglomeration of innovative workplaces, functions and productions, which until now have been growing, mainly spontaneously, also in the north-western sector of the Milan municipality (as the aforementioned Isola-Porta Garibaldi-Porta Nuova (Figure 1.8) and Bovisa-Dergano districts). At the same time, these two interventions might favour the further growth of the Milan urban region as main Italian node of a knowledge-based and creative economy through innovative (public and private) collaborations aimed at developing advanced services and specialized productions. However, the failure of the 1980s Bicocca Tecnocity project (Morandi, 2007) should be taken strongly into account.

Conclusion

Despite the future Metropolitan Territorial Plan will not include the outer part of the urban region, that overcomes the administrative borders of the Milan Metropolitan City, it should be able to coordinate the new trans-scalar centralities along the Milan north-west radial axis (at least) with the ones in other sectors of the urban core: for example, the future "City of Health and Research" in Sesto San Giovanni[21] (Figure 1.6) and the necessary reconfiguration of the historical university campuses (Figure 1.7). At the same time, by parallelly involving large projects that require time to be completed in an economically-sustainable way, this new plan should be flexible and incremental, by including both permanent and temporary uses (Bruzzese and Di Vita, 2016).

In order to develop a necessary broad and shared vision, for instance through the announced Strategic Agenda of the Metropolitan City, the performance of the local governance – whose lack has been one of the reasons behind Milan's incomplete metamorphosis into a world city (Bolocan Goldstein and Bonfantini, 2007) – must be improved. Accordingly, the northwestern sector of the Milan urban region could represent an interesting field of experimentation, beginning with the exploitation and upgrade of already existing (but sometimes weak) experiences of interistitutional cooperation. From the "Patto per il Nord Ovest Milano" – involving the Municipalities of the Rho area (Figure 1.6) – to the "Patto per l'Alto Milanese" – involving the Municipalities of the Legnano area (Figure 1.3) – in order to share services and policies.

Notes

1 See Chapters 1 and 2.
2 Formed by medium-sized cities such as Legnano, Busto Arsizio, Gallarate, and other minor towns.
3 See Chapter 2.
4 Homogeneous area (136 sqkm and 315,000 inhabitants) formed by Rho and other 15 Municipalities.
5 Homogeneous area (215 sqkm and 260,000 inhabitants) formed by Legnano and other 21 Municipalities.
6 From the economic point of view, whilst during the 2001–2011 period the average dynamics of local units registered +9.72 per cent in Italy, +10.62 per cent in the Milan urban region and +11.02 per cent in the Milan Metropolitan City, in the Milan municipal area it was +12.50 per cent, but in the "Nord Ovest" homogeneous area it was +8.70 per cent and in the "Alto Milanese" one it was +9.66 per cent. At the same time, whilst the average dynamics of employees registered +2.95 per cent in Italy, +2.69 per cent in the Milan urban region and +5.03 per cent in the Milan Metropolitan city, in the Milan municipal area it was +9.17 per cent, but in the "Nord Ovest" homogeneous area it was -6.53 per cent and in the "Alto Milanese" one it was -1.05 per cent (Centro Studi Pim, 2016).
7 See Chapter 7.
8 Followed by Ceretti & Tanfani and Origoni (mechanic industries), Broggi-Izar (metal industry), and Branca (liquor industry).
9 See Chapter 9.
10 This selection of projects refers to the following sources: Bolocan and Bonfantini, 2007; Morandi, 2007; Bolocan, Botti and Pasqui, 2011.
11 The Milan association of industrial firms.
12 See Chapter 5.
13 See Chapters 4 and 5.
14 Approved by the Milan Municipality in 1984 and 2000, respectively (See Chapter 1).
15 Approved by the Milan Metropolitan City in 2016.
16 See Chapter 9.
17 See Chapter 10.
18 See Chapter 7.
19 See Chapter 6.
20 Devoted to the digitization of the health sector.
21 See Chapter 7.

References

Balducci, A., Fedeli, V. and Cognetti, F. eds. (2010). *Milano: La città degli Studi, Storia, geografia e politiche delle università milanesi.* Milano: Abitare Segesta.

Balducci, A., Fedeli, V. and Curci, F. eds. (2017). *Post-metropolitan territories: Looking for a new urbanity.* London, New York: Routledge.

Boeri, S., Lanzani, A. and Marini, E. (1993). *Il territorio che cambia: Ambienti, paesaggi e immagini della regione urbana milanese.* Milano: Abitare Segesta.

Bolocan Goldstein, M. and Bonfantini, B. eds. (2007). *Milano incompiuta.* Milano: Franco Angeli.

Bolocan Goldstein, M., Botti, S. and Pasqui, G. eds. (2011). *Nord ovest Milano.* Milano: Electa.

Brenner, N. ed. (2014). *Implosions/explosions. Towards a study of planetary urbanization.* Berlin: Jovis Verlag.

Briata, P., Di Vita, S. and Pasqui, G. (2016). *Urban policy and responses to the crisis: The role of Academic and Research Institutions in Milan.* Paper presented at the *Eura Conference in Turin,* 16–18 June.

Bruzzese, A. and Di Vita, S. eds. (2016). Expo 2015 and its legacies. *Territorio,* 77, pp. 67–109.

Bruzzese, A. and Tamini, L. (2014). *Servizi commerciali e produzioni creative.* Milano: Bruno Mondadori.

Centro Studi PIM. (2016). Spazialità metropolitane: Economia, società territorio. *Argomenti e Contributi,* 15, Special Issue.

Erba, V., Molon, M. and Morandi, C. (2000). *Bovisa. Una riqualificazione possibile.* Milano: Unicopli.

Guallart, V. (2012). *The self-sufficient city.* New York City: Actar.

Hall, P. and Pain, K. eds. (2006). *The polycentric metropolis: Learning from megacity regions in Europe.* London: Earthscan.

Knieling, J. and Othengrafen, F. (2016). *Cities in crisis.* London, New York: Routledge.

Mariotti, I., Pacchi, C. and Di Vita, S. (2017). Coworking spaces in Milan: Location patterns and urban effects. *Journal of Urban Technology,* 24:3. Available online: http://www.tandfonline.com/doi/full/10.1080/10630732.2017.1311556.

Morandi, C. (2007). *Milan. The great urban transformation.* Venezia: Marsilio.

Perulli, P. (2014). Milan in the age of global contract. *Glocalism,* 3, pp. 1–16.

Scott, A.J. ed. (2001). *Global city-regions: Trends, theory, policy.* Oxford: Oxford University Press.

Soja, E.W. (2011). Regional urbanization and the end of the metropolis era. In: G. Bridge and S. Watson, eds., *The new companion to the city.* Hoboken, NJ: Wiley-Blackwell, pp. 679–689.

Taylor, P.J. (2004). *World city network: A global urban analysis.* London, New York: Routledge.

9 Territorial infrastructures and new production places

Andrea Rolando

Introduction

This contribution takes as its starting point the analysis of the natural and artificial networks that have supported the growth of Milan as a node of European relevance and that today constitute the framework for many actions of metropolitan governance. The mapping of these new and renewed tangible and intangible networks within the Milan urban region explain the effective and potential role of nodal places and their mutual connections inside and outside the metropolitan area, with specific focus on the places of location and development of new productions and economic activities.

Geographic and historic premises for understanding the current framework

The first physical component of the Milan urban region is the water system, with natural rivers and artificial canals as sources of energy and as transportation ways. The natural layer is mainly defined by the Alpine ridge with Lakes Maggiore and Como, powerful reservoirs of water and rich cultural hinges between the north and the south of the Alps. From the lakes, the Ticino and Adda rivers find their way, defining the natural and administrative borders of the Milan Metropolitan City on its eastern and western sides, together with smaller rivers (Seveso, Olona, Lambro), to end their course in the River Po on the southern side (Figure 1.2 and 1.3).

Another natural factor, still strictly related to physical geography and the water system, that is important to take into consideration is that the densest urban core of the wider urban region, while not touched by the main rivers, is still rich in underground waters and resurgences (*fontanili*) that emerge on the surface of the soil in parts of the city located south of a line (*linea delle risorgive*) defined by geomorphology and evident as a geographical pattern across the whole Po Valley (Turri, 2004). This line actually passes through the centre of Milan along the east-west axis, and water tends to naturally resurface south of it. Therefore, historically, the main industrial activities have been located in the northern sector of the metropolitan area, which is less suitable for agricultural purposes and today almost completely built over. In the southern sector, meanwhile, the soil and open spaces have traditionally been more carefully looked after and preserved, also thanks to the continuous presence of valuable agricultural usage. Even today, the balance between nature, man-made artefacts and the exploitation of resources is one of the main characteristics of the southern part of the metropolitan area of Milan, as demonstrated by the rural park of "Parco Agricolo Sud".

Another component in the territorial structure is the presence of the Alpine passes that have contributed to define the main infrastructural axes between the northern and the southern sides of the European continent.

Today, this network of historical routes is the focus of attentive care and preservation and is of particular interest as a basic layer suited to supporting a better sustainable relationship between such connections that belong to both the "long" (but slow) networks and the, for some aspects, similarly "long" (but fast) networks of the new European corridors, made by motorways and high-speed railways.

Starting out from the premises outlined above, the case study of the city of Milan, with its metropolitan area and urban region, is of particular interest for its role as the major city of the Po Valley. The Lombard capital emerges from a system of medium-sized and small cities, where different entities overlap to create a complex layered landscape, and where the infrastructure pertinent to the "long and fast" network of European corridors (Figures 1.1 and 1.2) coexists with:

- historical paths across the Alps (Via Francigena, Via Renana), which have today returned to play an important role as tourist paths, based also on values that strengthen the immaterial connections across Europe;
- a powerful capillary network of "short and slow" regional railways conceived and built in the years 1850–1930s, integrated with the new motorways and high-speed railways along the European corridors (Figures 1.2 and 1.3);
- a system of parks along the rivers, and other unique protected areas, such as the remains of the original forest of the Po plain (still present around the Ticino River);
- the Parco Agricolo Sud and other protected areas;
- important super-places, such as factories, shopping malls, logistic poles, data centres, airports (Linate, Malpensa, Orio al Serio), and exhibition venues (from the Milan Trade Fair to the Expo 2015 site) (Figures 1.3, 1.6, and 1.8).

These structural conditions provide a concrete opportunity for reconnecting and rethinking the whole landscape and producing a new kind of green infrastructure, considering the mobility networks and the in-between leftover spaces as the most meaningful places for intervention, even with projects based on improving the existing physical – natural and artificial – asset.

The interrelationship of the various geographic features has, in fact, deeply influenced the form of the Milan urban region and its characteristic balance between natural resources and productive landscapes, in a nodal position in a network of linear (rivers, canals, roads, and railways) components. The presence of rich natural and productive landscapes (agricultural and industrial) and their thorough integration with the infrastructural system offers today the opportunity to produce territorial innovation through functional and spatial design actions.

These components comprise the main structural, natural, and artificial realities, which, in the main, correspond to linear, radial systems that cross the whole urban region, enter as spines into the city and mark it from its core to its most peripheral outskirts. In the past, they powerfully influenced the city's fate; today they are the key components shaping Milan's urban form, and they are important for understanding the role of this city as an urban pole in the Italian industrial landscape and as one of the main urban nodes at the European scale.[1]

At the same time, this framework is the base layer that has defined the location of the most relevant interventions that have shaped the city's development.

The examples of the north-western sector in Milan (with the large redevelopment areas of Bovisa, the Farini railway yard, and Stephenson, as well as City Life, Portello, the Expo site, and Arese along the former Olona river bed),[2] the eastern sector (from Lambrate station to the city of Brescia) and the southern corridor (from Porta Romana station to the city of Abbiategrasso and to Ticino park) are important cases (Figure 1.6).

Spatial and functional features of the main nodes of the infrastructural network within the current process of urban change

As outlined above, the infrastructural node of Milan is historically characterized by a radial structure, with several networks converging on the main centre both from the urban region and from national and international directions (Figures 1.2 and 1.3).

Today it is possible to assume that the whole infrastructural system is almost complete and mature, at least as far as its functional purposes, and that four processes are taking place:

•   the spatial structure is facing a phase of transformation, turning from a fully radial system concentrated on the main node of Milan into a multipolar and pass-through model, with its scale being converted from only an urban or at most regional level, into a national and even international one;

- the nodes have consolidated their geographic role both in the neighbourhood and in the urban region, but their functional character is changing, from mainly industrial and infrastructural into a new and more multifunctional and complex role;
- information and communication technologies are changing the way urban polarities are located in the city, between tangible and intangible networks (Morandi, Rolando and Di Vita, 2016);
- the whole network is slowly upgrading, with better integration and spatial improvements in the punctual nodes and along the linear connections, improving the landscape's spatial quality along the banks of the infrastructure and in correspondence with the stations as public nodes.

This necessary development and upgrading of the system is in fact already taking place, though slowly and partially, generally along the main line corresponding to a great arc ranging from north-west to south-east, a kind of backbone of the contemporary development of Milan related to the infrastructure (Figures 1.6, 1.7, and 1.8). This new spatial component of the urban form of Milan is materializing along the high-speed line between the metropolitan municipalities of Rho (with the station of Rho Fiera) and San Donato (with the station of Milano Rogoredo), passing by Bovisa and Lambrate, which are to be considered, at the same time, nodes of the infrastructural and industrial genotype of the city and as a neighbourhood or district. Such a process of overall urban refurbishment is also echoing and extending its positive effects on branches of the systems at the urban and metropolitan level:

- to the west and Albairate, passing from Porta Romana and Porta Genova urban stations;
- to the north, from Bicocca former industrial site (Pirelli and Breda, now transformed into a new centrality with the University of Milan Bicocca and other main urban functions) to the metropolitan city of Sesto San Giovanni with the huge area of the Falck steel plant, now undergoing a complex urban remodelling;
- to the east, from Lambrate to Pioltello, where the new high-speed line has been extended to Brescia (completed in December 2016) and Venice (Figures 1.6, 1.7, and 1.8).

The former main industrial production plants of Pirelli, Breda, Falk in the north-eastern sector,[3] Alfa Romeo (Arese and Portello) and Candiani in the north-western,[4] as well as Innocenti, Ansaldo, and many other satellite enterprises spread around the city, which occupied vast portions of the densest urban core of the urban region and of its outskirts (Figure 1.6), are today nodes of the urban transformation that carry at the same time the image of historical heritage (to be integrated and preserved) and the opportunities for the development of new activities related to innovation of production methods, where the combination between work, life, education, mobility, spatial quality, and leisure are the key ingredients.

Some cases have anticipated the process, with the examples of the urban regeneration districts of Lambrate-Ventura and Porta Genova-Tortona[5] with the new MuDeC museum, a contemporary grafting on the former Ansaldo site. Similarly, the cases of Fondazione Prada at Porta Romana[6] and Fondazione Pirelli at Bicocca in Pirelli Hangar are to be considered as anticipations of this undergoing complex phase of urban change (Figure 1.8), capable of mixing the production and consumption of goods and services.

This process is taking place together with a general upgrading of the existing infrastructural mobility network – particularly with regards to the regional system – that has accompanied the process of upscaling and regionalizing urban productions and spaces, which has been occurring in Milan over the last 30 years.

The scale of this network, with good connections both within the Milan urban core and to the regional dimension (the so-called Passante network), has also created the opportunity for a different role of the same network, which is not only used for commuting between the metropolitan area centres of the hinterland and the main centre of Milan on weekdays; in recent years, there has been an increase in traffic during weekends of + 9.4 per cent,[7] and this is related to leisure, in both directions. The example of the Garbagnate station, connecting the park of metropolitan scale of Groane and the Expo site along the new canal of the "Via d'acqua",[8] is representative of this process, where an infrastructure apparently dedicated to leisure has in fact been realized as a new opportunity for the mobility system to also usefully connect up with a new urban node like the Expo site.

The processes briefly outlined in the previous paragraphs, together with the mix of physical and digital accessibility, the relationships to multiscalar networks, the presence of cultural and creative environments, the innovation produced by tangible and intangible networks and nodes in the process of evolution of contemporary metropolises are of great importance.

In this sense, at least six nodes of the infrastructural system of Milan, all to be considered as key places in the urban region, are worth mention and comment. Their importance is closely related to the geographic role they play at metropolitan, regional, or national and international level, and to their spatial relationship to their specific context, either because they are a component of a great urban transformation (Rho Fiera, Porta Garibaldi) or because they contribute as part of a smaller-scale diffused regeneration process (Bovisa, Lambrate, Porta Romana, Porta Genova) (Figures 1.6 and 1.7).

Among them, *Lambrate* and *Porta Genova* (Figures 1.6 and 1.8) seem to have already achieved a new role, integrating their functional position near two important Milan stations of the metropolitan railway network; their relationship to the water system (the Lambro River and the Martesana Canal for Lambrate, and the Naviglio Grande for Porta Genova); new attractive activities related to culture and leisure in the surrounding neighbourhoods; and light innovative production activities, possibly supported by digital processes.[9] Nevertheless, they can both be considered as lying within traditional urban transformation processes, even though strongly positioned on nodes of the mobility network.

On the other hand, four cases are paradigmatic of the new processes that are actually taking place, where the importance of each place is not only related to its functional role or to its position in the infrastructural system, but is also accompanied by a radical change in its geographic relevance, which is shifting from the urban or regional to the national or even international scale. Each place is not strictly to be considered as a punctual node, but more as a spatial element extended to a linear or areal spatial component of the metropolitan form of Milan.

The node of the station of *Bovisa-Villapizzone* is quite clear: it performs well as a mobility node of suburban and regional trains along the northwestern axis,[10] but it lacks better connections with the Politecnico university campus of Bovisa on the north side and with the existing neighbourhood on the south side of the railway line. The whole area, also through the new master plan for the gasometer area, could be improved, with better open spaces, green connections, and the settlement of new valuable activities, also in relation to the Farini railway yard tract, consequently creating the opportunity for a new, large, urban, green, and sustainable district (Figure 1.6).

On the other hand, the node of *Porta Garibaldi* has recently completed its transformation from a functional node, having abandoned warehouse spaces and other maintenance grounds, to a complex multiscalar node where different layers coexist: high-speed trains, regional and suburban trains, metro services, and local connections, where the whole mobility system is now running almost completely underground and the surface has been carefully redeveloped and integrated with the existing city through the new central pole of Porta Nuova (Figure 1.6).

The new metropolitan centrality around the railway station of *Rho Fiera*,[11] a node of great accessibility interchanging with Line 1 of the underground network and with the metropolitan, regional and high-speed railway (the latter open only during large-scale events), is a place that overcomes the urban and even the metropolitan level to establish its importance on the national and international scale, characterized by greater complexity and functional importance, as well as by high attractiveness due to its multimodal accessibility (Paris, 2009). In this area, where the Fiera venue is well established, the former Expo site is going to be transformed into the new science and technology park of the "Human Technopole" (Figure 1.6).

The last case of *Porta Romana* is located along a linear connection between the urban core high-speed train station of Milano Rogoredo and the local station of Abbiategrasso (next to Ticino River) in the western sector of the Milan Metropolitan city. It has created the opportunity for a new linear park, stretching along the Naviglio Grande between the Ticino river park and the node of Rogoredo, potentially to be extended across the new park of Forlanini to the airport of Linate, creating an innovative concept of coexistence between infrastructure and green (Figure 1.6).

The recent opening of the Fondazione Prada[12] (Figure 1.8), located next to the bundle of under-used tracks, has already started a new process of urban regeneration, suitable for the location of new production places thanks to the opportunities given by the presence of many small former industrial sites, well innervated with potential connections (that contribute to a better spatial quality) to one important component of the metropolitan area of Milan: the southern urban region rural park of the Parco Agricolo Sud. The presence of the abandoned railway area, with many unattended fringe areas between the railway and the surrounding city, to be accepted as a positive contribution to a "third" landscape (Clement, 2004), consolidates the role of the railway network as a hinge between the city and the countryside. The open spaces along the Vettabbia River, reaching the waste-water treatment plant of Nosedo, and the rediscovery of the old historical paths that connect the city centre and the open spaces with their networks of farms and abbeys in the outskirts surrounding Milan represent important opportunities, unique for the southern sectors of the city, for refurbishing and regenerating the whole area and for creating social innovation and building new relationships between the city, new productions and the countryside.

The interesting point, in the latter cases, is the attention to spatial quality and the creation of new open spaces (i.e., urban agriculture, allotments, informal gardens, pedestrian and cycle paths) capable of sewing – both functionally and spatially – and reconnecting the neighbourhood with the outskirts. But, mostly, it is important to consider their potential in terms of multiscalarity, that is, the potential of these places to produce new geographies and upscale the relationships between the site and the metropolitan area or even the region, establishing new relationships, at different speeds and with multimodal transportation opportunities, with the scale of the metropolitan region.

Upgrading the nodes and the brownfields of the infrastructural network into a system of green spaces to enable the location of innovative production sites

If we extend our view beyond the infrastructural network (canals, railways, roads), we may notice that, today, the Milan urban region is still characterized by vast portions of open spaces, more fragmented in the north, more continuous in the south. As outlined in the first section, these are both natural, especially along the rivers, or exploited for agricultural purposes. They are well organized, well maintained and, in fact, considered as parks, either because they are formally protected or because they are being used as leisure areas and therefore included within public and private actions of informal attention and care, responding to an increasingly pressing demand from inhabitants (insiders) and "users", mainly inhabitants of Milan who look for leisure spaces that are missing inside the core of the metropolitan area.

Furthermore, the infrastructural and industrial framework has left behind, as a weak heritage that needs to be considered, several – from middle to even small size – fringe areas, like those between the built centres, their peripheries and the countryside, the borders of the infrastructures, the industrial settlements, or the areas surrounding shopping centres, which are dramatically lacking in terms of spatial design.

A strong impulse to redesign these splintered and scattered places is now starting to drive strategic action, integrating the role of public and private actors (though still lacking any public formal support), with the aim of improving spatial quality as a basic condition for offering better functional opportunities. Above all, it is essential to redefine the role of the infrastructural system as a positive element in a complex landscape, considering at the same level, with a shot/countershot approach, how the space is perceived both by travellers moving along it and by the inhabitants/users of the crossed territories. The spatial quality of the places of interface would, therefore, be improved between the infrastructure and its environment (natural, agricultural, and built), like the "banks" of the motorways and railways, the stations on the regional railways network and the service areas placed along the main road and motorways, all of them to be considered as urban nodes that act as hinges between the built and the unbuilt components of the metropolitan area.

To consider the Milan urban region as a place of experimentation of a new kind of interaction space between infrastructure, open spaces, and new places of production is possible, also in light of the fact that the event of Expo 2015 in Milan produced, as a positive legacy, a new geographic placement of the Expo site, which has achieved a more central role, also in the collective perception.

Some specific cases, also located outside the metropolitan area of Milan, anticipate new relationships between landscape, infrastructure, and the location of new productions: the new Human Technopole in the former Expo site with the Fiera in Rho; the City of Healthcare in the former Flack industrial site of Sesto San Giovanni; the implementation of the high-tech district related to the Politecnico in the Bovisa gasometers, and the whole node of Rogoredo with its – still ongoing – development (Figure 06 and 07). These are all examples of interventions that for dimensions, functions, impacts, relationships to infrastructure, and multiscalar relationships between urban and regional scale are paradigms that should be an essential component of any strategic planning action and future vision.[13]

The process of upgrading, particularly within the Milan urban core, takes place at three integrated levels. The first two are related to spatial factors: to volumes of buildings and the surfaces of railway yards and other brownfields. For example, former logistic services or production plants that have positioned themselves in relation to the infrastructures, today abandoned but that have, in many cases, acquired, not only for those of high architectural value, an appealing patina of time and an important role as real-estate assets. Similarly, the abandoned areas mainly located along linear components of the metropolitan landscape today offer important opportunities for creating new connections and networks of green corridors along the banks of infrastructures where the original process of industrialization has taken place.

The presence of such valuable assets (attractive buildings and environments, potentially high-quality open spaces, strategic location along radial axes that connect centre and periphery well) is creating today (or recreating) new opportunities of location for innovative places of work. They are emerging from a reorganization of previous activities or from the acquisition of under-used spaces by new entrepreneurs, who often valorize them through informal, sometimes artistic, interventions (shared spaces for living, working, leisure activities) frequently based on the location of new formats of production spaces (fab labs, incubators). They are strongly supported by the social interaction of digital communities and activate processes that are based on tangible and intangible values that can at the same time establish a fundamental spatial cohesion that, in the end, produces positive spatial effects.

Conclusion

As previously seen, the infrastructural system of Milan has supported the definition and growth of the city's urban form throughout its many various phases: the first and second based on the exploitation of water resources and on the realization of the canals (fourteenth to nineteenth century) ended with the completion of the railway networks. Together they supported the first industrial revolution, which also corresponded to the process of the Unification of Italy, with a national government. A third phase was based on the construction of the networks of motorways and more diffused means of transportation, culminating in the economic boom of the 1960s. All together, they have generated Milan's territorial system of nodes and connections and strongly defined its urban form and that of the metropolitan area. However, while the first two outlined an evident relationship between infrastructure and the location of vast industrial sites, the latter supported the more chaotic, independent, medium- and small-size activities, producing the scattered sprawl of the contemporary urban region.

Today, as the system is mostly complete and mature, an overall improvement and upgrading process is occurring, based on a new relationship between infrastructure and ecology, combining the railway networks and the implementation of parks and open spaces to build a green infrastructure: both are key requirements for the localization of new productions. Now, the main challenge is to rethink a new kind of infrastructure, a combination of the traditional "blue" layer with rivers and canals into a new concept of green infrastructure, which can be given such a name because it was formed as an infrastructure in the true sense. Today, this can be transformed into a blue-green system based on canals and green corridors integrated with the mobility network. At the same time, the new nodes of the high-speed railway are changing the form and the scale of the metropolitan area, defining new places and new geographies.

Moreover, in present and future years, a new layer of intangible networks and actions is being added to the historical ones that defined the shape of Milan and that are now being adapted to a new geography. This new layer seems to be supporting and enhancing the physical refurbishment strategy. This is also due to recent developments deriving from the concept of digital smartness, which aims to redefine the ideas of place and centrality, creating an analogy between the virtual network of Internet sites and the physical network of places. In this sense, the metropolitan shape of Milan is tending to break out and spill over its administrative borders, extending processes and actions from the urban scale to the regional one (Morandi, Rolando and Di Vita, 2016), by experimenting the use of information and communications technologies and specific digital services in marginal places as a tool to integrate traditional spatial design actions, so to enable the location of new productions and activities, create better living conditions, and contribute to better relationships between people and places. Thanks to the role played by infrastructure and its relationship with open green spaces, this is happening not only in the urban core, but also in the in-between territories that separate the main metropolitan centre of Milan and the cities of the mega-city region along the Po Valley, creating new geographies from Turin to Trieste, including the old industrial triangle Turin-Milan-Genoa and the linear urban system stretching along the Adriatic coast.

Notes

 1 See Chapter 2.
 2 See Chapter 8.
 3 See Chapter 7.
 4 See Chapter 8.
 5 See Chapter 4.
 6 See Chapters 4 and 6.
 7 Trenord 2015 Social Report www.trenord.it/it/chi-siamo/l-azienda/bilancio-sociale.aspx.
 8 The new canal, the so called "Via d'acqua" (Waterway) was built as part of the Expo project, to bring water to the site and to create a new green connection between the Villoresi Canal north of Milan and the Naviglio Grande in the south of the city. The last part, from the Expo site to the Naviglio Grande, has not been realized.
 9 See Chapter 4.
10 See Chapter 8.
11 See Chapter 8.
12 See Chapter 6.
13 In addition to these urban and metropolitan innovative nodes that enable new productions, some that refer to the macro regional scale could be listed, all located in the territories that are affected by the changes related to the process of upgrading the infrastructural system and the railway high-speed network.
   For example, on the axis of the European corridor 5: the production and research centre of Km Rosso; the recent discussed location of Percassi headquarters in the UNESCO site of Crespi d'Adda; the factory of Artemide; the logistic pole and the research center of Novamont in Novara; the logistic pole of Vicolungo; the factories of Sambonet, Gessi and Alessi of the home design district; and the new factories of Pirelli, Aurora, Lavazza and L'Oreal in the Turin metropolitan area facing Milan.
   On the axis to Bologna, the logistics settlements of IKEA and Amazon near Piacenza.

References

Assolombarda, Unione Industriale di Torino e Confindustria Genova, Osservatorio Territoriale del Nord Ovest. (2016). *Dossier sul nodo metropolitano di Milano.*
Bolocan Goldstein, M., Botti, S. and Pasqui, G. eds. (2011). *Nord Ovest Milano.* Milan: Electa.
Clement, G. (2004). *Manifeste du Tiers paysage.* Paris: Sujet/Objet.
Morandi, C. (2007). *Milan: The great urban transformation.* Venice: Marsilio.
Morandi, C., Rolando, A. and Di Vita, S. (2016). *From smart city to smart region, digital services for an internet of places.* Cham: Springer.
Paris, M. (2009). *Urbanistica dei superluoghi.* Sant'Arcangelo di Romagna: Maggioli.
Rolando, A. (2016). Untying the knot of the expo site, a multiscalar node between urban and regional scales. *Territorio,* 77, pp. 87–90.
Turri, E. (2004). *La Megalopoli Padana.* Venice: Marsilio.

10 The last cycle of Milan urban policies and the prospects for a new urban agenda

Gabriele Pasqui

Introduction

In recent years, the consequences of the global crisis have particularly affected the Southern European cities (Aalbers, 2009; Knieling and Othengrafen, 2016), with economic recession, increasing unemployment rates, and welfare cuts. Milan has, as have other European cities (URBACT, 2010), explored approaches and tools to tackle the crisis effects.

In July 2016, Giuseppe Sala – former CEO of the Expo 2015 management company – was elected Mayor of Milan, supported by a centre-left coalition. He replaced Giuliano Pisapia, who was the first left-wing Mayor after almost 20 years of right-wing administrations. The Sala's agenda aims at continuing that of Pisapia, confirming a radical change in the Milan political context. This change has influenced not only the urban policies, but also visions, narratives, discourses, and priorities of the urban agenda.

In Europe and Italy, the discussion about urban agendas (European Union, 2011; Calafati, 2014; Pasqui, 2017) is closely linked to the new global challenges (climate change, new forms of spatial inequalities, effects of economic crisis: Cities Alliance, 2015), as well as to the redefinition of urban policies at the EU level (EU Council, 2016). Accordingly, this concluding chapter shows how the last cycle of Milan's urban policies was affected by economic and social changes, and what challenges arise in defining a new agenda for not only the Milan municipal area, but its wider urban region.

Economic crisis, political change, and urban agenda

Over the last 10 years, Milan has been subject to a complex interaction among political and socio-economic cycles that changed the urban agenda after a long period of stability (Pasqui, 2011). The 2008 economic crisis hit Milan and its urban region in four main ways. The first one was the stagnation of the urban market, which interrupted the long positive real estate cycle, halting or redefining many relevant urban development projects.[1] Whilst the property values remained at high levels, the credit crunch made it harder to access mortgage-financed homeownership. This directly affected the housing affordability of a growing proportion of families, leading in worst cases to evictions and repossessions (Nomisma, 2016).

The second dynamic was the uprising of new socio-spatial inequalities, and the growing social fragility for many families and individuals – especially in some areas of the urban region – thus confirming the potential trade-off between cohesion and competitiveness in a phase of economic crisis (Cucca and Ranci, 2017).

The third one was the local finance crisis, with a dramatic reduction in resources for local authorities (especially municipalities), resulting in a reduction of public services (Costa and Sabatinelli, 2013).

The final consequence was the crisis (and sometimes bankruptcy) suffered by many companies in the industrial, service, and retail sectors, resulting in unemployment and growing insecurity regarding employment contracts (Centro Studi PIM, 2016).

Even though these effects of the global crisis, during the decade 2006–2016, Milan was one of few Italian cities to face the crisis with broadly encouraging performances (Camera di Commercio di Milano, 2016). For instance, its metropolitan area was characterized by a low level of unemployment compared to that of other Italian cities; several new firms set up business in its urban region; tourist flows increased, also thanks to the Expo 2015 (that attracted more than 20 million visitors).

What are the reasons behind this performance? First, Milan has always been characterized by an un-specialized and multiple economic base, with an important role played by different economic clusters (Foot, 2001). This is the reason why the last ten years have resulted in a high establishment rate of businesses and an interesting development of new forms of entrepreneurship.[2] Second, Milan is an international city; it is the only Italian city capable of attracting highly skilled human capital and relevant foreign direct investments – not only in the real estate sector. Third, Milan institutions were able to promote a new attractiveness of the city, contributing to change its image and social perception for tourists, buyers, and investors. Therefore, the interaction between politics, policies, and economic dynamics has been crucial in strengthening the Milan urban region's response to the crisis.

Before and after the crisis

The new urban agenda promoted by the left-wing administration under Mayor Giuliano Pisapia partially continues while partially discontinuing the one that the previous right-wing Mayor Letizia Moratti promoted during her mandate (2006–2011).

Around 2006, Milan was a city characterized by a complex and pluralistic governance system, in which many actors played an important role: from the Chamber of Commerce to universities, from banking foundations to organized civil society (associations, third sector, non-profit enterprises). Over the years, this complex network was able to produce resources and projects built without (and sometimes against) the public administration (Dente et al., 2005).

In this context, Mayor Moratti also inherited a substantial continuity of the urban agenda. The issues subject to focus were still those of modernization that characterized the 1980s (Bolocan Goldstein and Pasqui, 2011). The main issues addressed by the Moratti administration were support for economic transition by creating large scale urban projects (in particular, through the reuse of large brownfield sites), the strengthening of large infrastructure networks (primarily roads and new railways), and improved administrative efficiency through a progressive outsourcing of public services. Moreover, close attention was paid to the rising question of security, often connected to the problematic governance of migration phenomena.

Compared to the previous two decades, the previous right-wing administrations of the late 1990s and early 2000s under Mayor Gabriele Albertini were characterized by their ability to complete projects and public works. Between 1998 and 2006, after a block in construction, some important infrastructural projects designed and programmed in the 70s and 80s were completed; from the Passante Ferroviario to Line 3 of the subway. At the same time, a strong pro-growth coalition led to the conditions of a real estate over-production (Figure 1.6), the effects of which would be felt throughout the next decade.

In 2008–2009, after the initial phase of Moratti's administration, the urban market crisis started to influence strongly socio-economic dynamics. Milan had, in fact, already fully completed its economic transition to post-Fordism which had started in the 1970s. From a demographic point of view, Milan had become a smaller city (the decline of the population between 2001 and 2011 also affected other metropolitan municipalities which were the main ones hit by the counter-urbanization of the 1980s and 1990s), became older and more fragmented (with an incredible number of single-member families), and more multiethnic (Centro Studi PIM, 2016).

Milan – never exclusively a manufacturing city – had already redefined the profile and characteristics of the service sectors, highlighting its strong ability to play an important role in the international division of labour in the field of high value-added services, operating as a "node of the global network" (Magatti, 2005). Over the decades, Milan had consolidated a leading role not only in the already established chains of finance, fashion, and design, but also in those of health and biomedical research, higher education and training, and high value-added businesses. As in other phases, the city showed strong resilience against structural changes.

Nevertheless, if the transition from industrial to tertiary Milan, between 1980 and 2000, was based on the economics of high value added services, fashion and design clusters, and of the role of the real estate sector, the 2008 crisis redefined the development model and challenged the actors to re-invent a development pattern based on new economies.

From the second phase of the Moratti administration (2009–2011), despite the absence of a collapse in real estate values, the urban market and its actors began to have great difficulty in ensuring the resources and investments to complete several large scale redevelopment projects. Some of the most important developers operating in Milan were stifled by debts and were forced to leave in the hands of creditor banks or other Italian and international developers large projects initiated in the previous phase (Porta Vittoria, Santa Giulia, the Falck area in Sesto San Giovanni). More generally, the market dynamics showed an overproduction, especially in the segment of high-range residences, but also in the directional tertiary field. The same difficulties of two crucial and central projects such as Porta Nuova and City Life showed the existence of a real estate bubble, difficult to plan and control (Figure 1.6).

Faced with these effects of the crisis, the Moratti administration tried to support the real estate market, relaxing planning rules with a new pro-growth master plan (Piano di Governo del Territorio – PGT). In this sense, the PGT adopted shortly before the 2011 elections set up a real estate development policy that was inadequate for market dynamics, as it tried to bring people into the city, but also to promote international projects based on designs by many global architects (Zaha Hadid, Daniel Libeskind, Cesar Pelli, Arata Isozaki, Stefano Boeri, and others).

This strategy was also favoured by the nomination of and subsequent award to the Expo 2015, which opened up a unique opportunity to return to the centre of the international stage (Pasqui, 2016).

It is in this context of strong uncertainty that the Giuliano Pisapia's centre-left political coalition won the municipal elections of May 2011, defeating Letizia Moratti with more than 55 per cent of votes. Giuliano Pisapia decided to support the Expo event and to strengthen the internationalization strategy launched by Moratti with the Expo candidature. On the other side, without reopening the planning process, the Pisapia administration started a revision of the PGT, introducing some significant changes to reduce the quantitative impact of urban transformations and proposing a more effective governance of the widespread transformations in the consolidated city.

Urban change and urban policies during the Pisapia administration

Faced with the public resources crisis, the Pisapia administration promoted greater transparency and accountability in the management of the public-private relationship, trying to guarantee transparency in public-private relationships and focusing on the reuse of abandoned or underused spaces located throughout the urban fabric.

On the other side, Pisapia was able to support the dynamism of civil society and the processes of social innovation, especially in the fields of creative productions[3] and sharing economies.[4]

Trying to manage the complex situation of interrupted large-scale urban development projects and to identify realistic strategies for new public areas such as underused railway areas or military barracks, the Pisapia administration was also able to support the spontaneous processes of urban change described in this book.

These molecular processes have produced important social and spatial changes in many different parts of Milan's densest urban core (Figure 1.8) and of its wider urban region, and in recent years the urban agenda has recognized the potential of these processes to redefine a new urban development model.

The approach of the Pisapia administration to these new processes of economic and social innovation was clear. During a shortage in public resources, the role of the Municipality was first of all to give immaterial support to the experiences promoted by the civil society and by the new makers, offering a platform for the exchange of information and a support to the spontaneous processes of networking and self-promotion (Comune di Milano and Fondazione Brodolini, 2016).

This approach promoted by the Pisapia administration was also closely linked to the focus on the direct participation of civil society in city life; this was one of the distinctive features of the Pisapia electoral program. Over the administration's five years, Mayor Pisapia was supported by self-organized civil society groups, who asked to actively participate in city government. In this context, a central point of the Pisapia agenda was to interact with these actors and to promote supporting policies that could strengthen social and entrepreneurial innovation.

Among the soft and enabling policies promoted by the Pisapia administration, especially thanks to the activism of the Deputy Major for Innovation Policies, Cristina Tajani, we can first of all cite the intervention on the temporary reuse of abandoned spaces that was able to provide new spaces and opportunities to many enterprises, associations, and local actors.

Other interesting policies promoted by the Milan Municipality were the support to self-organizing experiences of urban agriculture, intended both as a form of look after non-urbanized land as well as to promote neighbour-hood and community social relations; moreover, Municipality-supported networks of local actors interested in developing an integrated design of urban parks; mobility (bike and car) sharing; other experiences of peer2peer sharing.

All these initiatives were fuelled by the idea that social innovation and community mobilization may be part of a wider policy that tries to sup-port the private production of public goods. The policies that activated net-works and services for entrepreneurial experiences in neo-manufacturing and sharing economy, described in other chapters of this book, also moved in this direction. Moreover, relevant economic, cognitive, and symbolic resources were found for a program aimed at combining the theme of smart city with social innovation. In this sense, words like community welfare, sharing economy, social innovation, international openness, smart city, start up, FabLab, areas of co-working, smart working, and new forms of mutual-ism have become important elements in the policies promoted by the Pisa-pia administration, conjugating the themes of technological innovation with an approach focused on social cohesion.

Finally, after years characterized by a rather traditional dialogue between government and citizens, the Pisapia administration began working on public participation in decision-making and planning processes. Experi-ences like the Participatory Budget – in 2015 Milan decided to manage nine million euros of its budget through a participatory approach – or civic crowdfunding, a bottom-up fundraising program targeted at social innova-tion projects in the city and for the city, are in this sense experimental and limited but promising steps.

Another important aspect of the Pisapia administration was the promo-tion of events and activities that were able to open up the city to external visitors but also to its own citizens. Cultural initiatives such as Piano City or Book City, the use of some parts of underused railway areas for host-ing street food, commercial activities but also cultural initiatives during the Expo event, the opening of the Darsena in the Porta Genova-Tortona area, and many others were able to change the same perception of Milan. Prob-ably for the first time in years, Milan is currently on the map of the most vibrant European cities, attractive for tourists but also for skilled workers.

The attraction of skilled workers is connected with the policies promoted by other actors (for example, by universities) to strengthen internationaliza-tion and attractiveness.

In this perspective, this new image of the city may be considered part of a new urban agenda that is changing not only the attractiveness of the city, but also its development model. This urban agenda, for the first time, is able to identify the opportunities connected with the liveliness of Milanese civil society and socio-economic actors, and the possibilities offered by bottom-up social innovation experiences and experimentations. Moreover, this agenda is not only the effect of institutional strategies and public policies; it is the effect of the mobilization of a complex and pluralistic network of local and non-local actors.

On the other hand, it is important to underline two main critical questions that are currently only partially at the centre of the public agenda.

First, these innovative processes are mainly hosted in the city centre, while socio-economic processes and effects of the crisis affect the urban region. As we shall see, this depends also on the lack of an effective governance on the metropolitan level, even though a new metropolitan institution was established by a national law at the beginning of 2015.

Second, the innovative processes are often concentrated, spatially and socially, in some sectors of the city. Social problems (poverty, migration, security, lack of social services) have grown in recent years and are now concentrated in specific areas. The risk of socio-spatial polarization is rising and must be controlled.

The challenges of the metropolitan government

The metropolis is at the core of institutional reform in several European countries. One of the key questions is how administrative and political forms are designed to capture the socio-spatial relations represented by the urban dimension (Cole and Payre, 2016).

As required by national law no. 56/2014 (so called *Legge Delrio* named after the Minister who promoted it), the 1st January 2015 saw the formal establishment of the Milan Metropolitan City,[5] a new institution of metropolitan government (Fedeli, 2016). Having respected the time-scale defined by law, the new institution is now undergoing a problematic and uncertain start-up phase. The process leading to the approval of the Statute – which took place between October and December 2014 – marked an important step, but failed to address some very important issues.

There are three, among other, complications that indicate the distance between the provided solution (with the institutionalization of a metropolitan government) and the problems on the table. The first has to do with territorial delimitation, since the borders of the new Metropolitan City (Figure 1.3) are the same as the old and now abolished Milan Province. As many chapters of this book clearly show, these boundaries of the new metropolitan institution are not adequate in facing the complex policy issues whose boundaries are often larger[6] (Balducci, Fedeli and Curci, 2017).

The second relates to the governance model, which still provides that the Metropolitan Mayor is not elected directly by citizens and coincides with the Mayor of the Milan Municipality. This situation leads to potential intermunicipality conflicts, and to a limited legitimation of the metropolitan institution.

The third complication is the blurry definition of powers and responsibilities of the new metropolitan institution, in relation to the other institutions (the State, the Region, the Municipalities, and especially the central city) and the other stakeholders.

During 2013 and 2014, the approval of the *Delrio Law* and the process of establishing the Metropolitan City were preceded and accompanied by a limited debate. In particular, the involvement of civil society in the constitutional process was rather weak. Even the Expo, despite producing a significant case of identification of the largest urban region in the event, does not seem to have helped to qualify the debate. Public discussion still appears to have no real political leadership, as highlighted by the almost total absence of the theme in Milan's recent mayoral election campaign, the same as that of the Metropolitan City.

On the other hand, over the course of 2016 the establishment of the Boroughs in the Milan Municipality and of the Districts in the Milan Metropolitan City (inter-municipal homogeneous areas, built for managing public services), could allow for a renewal of the urban agenda. The Boroughs, in fact, may generate a new proximity between institutions and citizens, in particular on the issues of local services, habitability, and quality of life (Balducci, Fedeli and Pasqui, 2011); the districts of the new metropolitan government might constitute an effective means of planning cooperation on strategic issues between different municipalities.

Generally speaking, two years after the Metropolitan City was formally established, it is not possible to say that we have a consistent metropolitan agenda. While many of the territorial and economic issues addressed in this book at least have a metropolitan dimension, at this point we don't have a clear institutional governance platform to face and treat these issues.

Nevertheless, the start-up of the Metropolitan City could be facilitated if the new institution would invest more in enhancing cooperation practices. Different experiences of inter-municipal cooperation and inter-institutional partnership represent a reference point, even if the propulsive phase of voluntary inter-municipal cooperation in the Milan that grew in the second half of the 1990s is now weaker. However, best practices of cooperation in some fields of public policies (spatial planning, mobility and infrastructure, support for innovative activities, management of public services) that are crucial for the effectiveness of metropolitan governance, can be recognized in these experiences.[7]

For these reasons, the Metropolitan City needs to play a role promoting specific projects and actions of inter-municipal cooperation, as many other metropolitan areas have done over past decades. Themes such as the redevelopment and promotion of the post-Expo area, the management of the public transport system, the spatial reorganization of the sanitary cluster, the coordination among universities and research centres, support to new manufacturing services and areas should be at the very core of Metropolitan City activities.

Finally, the Metropolitan City should be able to show that its existence does not represent a new mechanism of government bureaucratization, but a tool to simplify and rationalize public action, also in the field of spatial planning, offering efficient services to citizens and municipalities. This is possible starting from the abandonment of costly competition between functions and territories, supplying innovative mechanisms in the field of territorial compensation.

A new metropolitan agenda, coherent with urban dynamics on the urban level, should be based on a policy of cooperation, able to produce projects through agreements and select initiatives and programs based on criteria of efficiency and effectiveness.

Conclusion

In the years of the Pisapia administration, a complex network of public, quasi-public, and private actors was able to produce new narratives on Milan. The attention shifted from a traditional pro-growth development model to a new mixed development pattern, based on the mobilization of society's intelligence, the internationalization and attraction of investments and talents, and the support for new entrepreneurial initiatives.

This new economic base was not only rooted in traditional fields of creativity, fashion, design, finance and biomedical clusters. Interesting experiences were promoted in fields of 4.0 manufacturing, art and culture, tourism, new urban agriculture, green economies. Whilst some of these experiences are still in the embryo stage, they are able to demonstrate that a new and sustainable socio-economic development pattern is possible.

In order to strengthen this new development model, policies and institutional arrangements are required, even though (at this moment) the new Metropolitan City seems unable to give the necessary institutional support. Moreover, within this uncertain institutional framework, the political coalition that supported Giuseppe Sala has been characterized by a substantial continuity with the experience of Pisapia. Nevertheless, the victory for a few thousand votes against its competitor took place in a climate of great uncertainty, demonstrating the persistence of problems and issues perceived by large sectors of society.

In particular, the perception of this Milan renewal, the uprising of a new optimism for the future of the city was mainly the sentiment of a small part of the Milanese society: for instance, young people, with a high level of human capital, involved in social innovation practices. Other parts of the local society refuse to recognize these changes: a fear of anything new and potentially dangerous (immigrants, refugees, crime), but also the crisis in local welfare, have produced a sense of social and spatial insecurity, mainly concentrated in some neighbourhoods of Milan and its metropolitan area.

A new urban agenda for Milan is, above all, an agenda that considers the importance of these narratives and sentiments and that tries to avoid polarization between Italian and foreign citizens, rich and poor, old and young, skilled and unskilled workers. For this reasons, the question of deprived areas and neighbourhoods (the "peripheries") is at this moment a central point of public debate.

The new agenda that the administration is trying to vehicle is based on a double narrative. On one hand, we recognize the need to consolidate, following Expo 2015, the internationalization process and the opening to the world. These objectives are pursued through appropriate strategies of internationalization, attraction of investments, and rare functions (up to the proposal, post-Brexit, to host European agencies located in London in Milan), the definition of major projects in the research and education sector (such as the Human Technopole project in the post-Expo area).

On the other hand, the slogan used by Sala ("Starting from the peripheries") means that the new administration and the new Mayor want to pay attention to issues of social cohesion, through support to the most disadvantaged populations who risk exclusion from regeneration and social innovation processes that have characterized recent years.

It is a strategy that seeks to balance inclusion and innovation, also referring to a long civic tradition. On the other hand, it is a very difficult challenge, between policies to support international competitiveness and consolidation measures of welfare and social inclusion there are also potential trade-offs. The policy-making capacity to limit these trade-offs and to interpret this double narrative through coherent and effective policies on the metropolitan level – connected to the manifold networks and actions at the urban region scale – is the only way to give adequate support to the complex processes of spatial and social innovation, in the context of multi-scalar and market pressures that are described in this book.

Notes

1 See Chapters 7 and 8.
2 See Chapters 1, 4, and 5.
3 See Chapter 4.
4 See Chapter 5.

5 In Italian, the *Città Metropolitana*.
6 See Chapter 2.
7 See also Chapters 7 and 8.

References

Aalbers, M.B. (2009).Geographies of financial crisis. *Area*, 41, pp. 34–42.
Balducci, A., Fedeli, V. and Curci, F. (2017). *Post-metropolitan territories and urban space*. London: Routledge.
Balducci, A., Fedeli, V. and Pasqui, G. (2011). *Strategic planning for contemporary urban regions*. London: Ashgate.
Bolocan Goldstein, M. and Pasqui, G. (2011). Oltre la crescita edilizia: Una nuova agenda pubblica per Milano. In: A. Arcidiacono, L. Pogliani, eds., *Milano al futuro: Riforma o crisi del governo urbano*. Milano: Et Al., pp. 270–304.
Calafati, A.G., ed. (2014). *Città, tra sviluppo e declino: Un'agenda urbana per l'Italia*. Roma: Donzelli.
Camera di Commercio di Milano. (2016). *Milano produttiva 2016*. Milano: Bruno Mondadori.
Centro Studi PIM. (2016). Spazialità metropolitane: Economia, società territorio. *Argomenti e Contributi*, 15, pp. 1–104.
Cities Alliance. (2015). *Sustainable development goals and Habitat III: Opportunities for a successful new urban agenda*. Discussion paper n° 3, Bruxelles, Adelphi and Urban Catalyst, Novembre. [online] Available at: www.citiesalli ance.org/sites/citiesalliance.org/files/Opportunities%20for%20the%20New%20 Urban%20Agenda.pdf.
Cole, A. and Payre, R. eds. (2016). *Cities as political objects: Historical evolution, analytical categorisations and institutional challenges of metropolitanisation*. Cheltenham: Edward Elgar.
Comune di Milano and Fondazione Brodolini. (2016). *Libro bianco sull'innovazione sociale*. Milano: Comune di Milano.
Costa, G. and Sabatinelli, S. (2013). *Wilco WP4 Milan report*. [online] Available at: www.wilcoproject.eu/wordpress/wp-content/uploads/WP-4-Milan.pdf.
Cucca, R. and Ranci, C. eds. (2017). *Unequal cities: The challenge of post-industrial transition in times of austerity*. London: Routledge.
Dente, B., Bobbio, L. and Spada A. (2005). Government or governance of urban innovation? A tale of two cities. *Disp, The Planning Review*, 162, pp. 41–53.
EU Council. (2016). *Urban agenda for the Eu "Pact of Amsterdam": Agreed at the informal meeting of Eu ministers responsible for urban matters on 30 may 2016 in Amsterdam*. The Netherlands. [online] Available at: http://urbanagendaforthe. eu/wp-content/uploads/2016/05/Pact-of-Amsterdam_v7_WEB.pdf.
European Union, Regional Policies. (2011). *Cities of tomorrow: Challenges, visions, ways forward*. Bruxelles: European Union.
Fedeli, V. (2016). Metropolitan governance and metropolitan cities in Italy: Outdated solutions for processes of urban regionalisation? *Raumforschung und Raumordnung*, 3, pp. 265–274.

Foot, J. (2001). *Milan since the miracle.* London: Bloomsbury Academic.

Knieling, J. and Othengrafen, F. eds. (2016). *Cities in crisis.* Abingdon: Routledge.

Magatti, M. et al. (2005). *Milano nodo della rete globale: Un itinerario di analisi e proposte.* Milano: Bruno Mondadori.

Nomisma. (2016). *9° Rapporto sulla finanza immobiliare.* Bologna: Nomisma.

Pasqui, G. (2011). The changing urban agenda. In: A. Balducci, V. Fedeli and G. Pasqui, eds., *Strategic planning for contemporary urban regions.* London: Ashgate, pp. 55–67.

Pasqui, G. (2016). Expo 2015 and Milan: Interwined stories. *Urbanistica,* 155, pp. 106–117.

Pasqui, G. (2017). *Le agende urbane delle città italiane: Secondo Rapporto Urban@ it.* Bologna: Il Mulino.

URBACT. (2010). *URBACT, Cities facing the crisis: Impact and responses.* [online] Available at: http://urbact.eu/files/urbact-cities-facing-crisis-impact-and-responses.

Index